GENERATIONS APART

GENERATIONS APART

by Peter Gordon

WARNER/CHAPPELL PLAYS

LONDON

A Warner Music Group Company

GENERATIONS APART
First published in 1996
by Warner/Chappell Plays Ltd
129 Park Street, London W1Y 3FA

ISBN 0 85676 157 5

Printed by Commercial Colour Press, London E7

Dedicated to the memory of my father, George Gordon

GENERATIONS APART has six characters, two of whom appear in both youth and middle-age.

PAUL: Late forties (1996 scenes)

AL: PAUL'S son, mid-twenties (1996 scenes)

PAUL: Early twenties (1969 scenes)

ALBERT: PAUL'S father, mid-fifties (1969 scenes)

OLIVE: PAUL'S mother, mid-fifties (1969 scenes)

ANNE: Late forties (1996 scenes)

JULIE: ANNE'S daughter, mid-twenties (1996 scenes)

ANNE: Early twenties (1969 scenes)

NB: The roles of YOUNG PAUL and AL may be played by
            the same actor, and the roles of YOUNG ANNE and
            JULIE by the same actress.

The action takes place on a cliff top on the Isle of Wight.

ACT ONE

Scene One: Summer, 1996.
Scene Two: Summer, 1969.

ACT TWO

Scene One: Summer, 1969, one week later.
Scene Two: 1996, several days after the
                events of Act One, Scene One.

During the interval and scene changes, music appropriate to the correct time period should be used to set the mood.

ACT ONE

Scene One

A cliff top on the Isle of Wight during summer, 1996. Upstage is a hedge which represents the boundary of the cliff top public footpath. Stage right is a wooden fence over which is a stile. Near the stile is a signpost which says "Footpath to Freshwater". Centre stage there is a wooden "park type" bench on which is affixed a small brass plaque. The beach and sea beyond are imagined to be in the auditorium.

As the opening music plays, PAUL *enters over the stile. He is in his late forties, has a tendency to be rather vague, but has the optimistic good humour of one who thinks that a victory against all the odds, although unlikely, is just possible. He is quite scruffily dressed in casual old-fashioned clothes. He carries a sports bag. Music fades.*

PAUL (*looking back*) Come on, Al, keep up will you!

(AL *appears and climbs very carefully over the stile. He is* PAUL'S *son and is in his mid-twenties. In contrast to* PAUL, *although casually dressed in a "jogging outfit", it is very much in a "designer" style. He regards himself as upwardly mobile and has a much greater sense of urgency and expectation than* PAUL.)

AL Have you been on anabolic steroids?

PAUL I can't walk any slower!

AL I'm stiff! I was playing squash last night.

PAUL If that's as fast as you can move I assume you lost!

AL I was playing with someone who might be able to put some business our way. I wasn't meant to win. God, I ache!

PAUL   I'm not expecting you to do a vault over the stile. Just try to generate some kind of forward momentum, that's all.

AL   Okay, I'm here, no sweat. (*Examining his clothes and finding a small mark.*) Oh hell, look at that! It's the first time I've worn this as well! (*Doing a few stretching exercises.*) I don't know why we're walking in the first place! I could have got the motor this far. Four wheel drive, foot on the floor . . . excellent!

PAUL   I happen to like walking. I know it's a rather outmoded form of transport but some people still get pleasure out of it.

AL   Takes all sorts doesn't it? Can't see the point of legs now we've invented the wheel . . . or maybe you hadn't noticed that the wheel has actually been invented. (*Examining the back of his clothes.*) Damn, it's all round the back. Cost a fortune as well. Do you think they'd change it?

PAUL   But would you get another romper suit in such a large size! I thought they only went up to age five.

AL   Do you mind, it's good stuff is this! (*Touching his toes.*) It's the label isn't it? You've got to wear the right label!

PAUL   Yeah, I suppose life's not worth living with the wrong label! (*Noticing* AL *and attempting in vain to touch his own toes.*) I used to be able to do that.

AL   Callisthenics?

PAUL   (*dubious*) Perhaps I couldn't then. (*Sitting on the bench, thoughtful.*) Somebody could make a fortune out of just producing the right designer labels . . . you could stick them on anything. (*He pulls out a handkerchief and polishes the brass plaque.*)

AL (*serious*) You might have a point there.

PAUL I was joking! It would be illegal, Al.

AL There'd be ways around it . . . just the modern way of doing business. Sure, you've got to duck and dive a bit . . .

PAUL Duck and dive?

AL Yeah . . . bob and weave. I know how to play the angles, you don't.

PAUL (*in exasperation, more to himself than to* AL) Bob and weave, play the angles? I don't know if I've raised a boxing champ, a snooker king or just a complete moron!

AL (*imitating a punch drunk boxer*) I could've been a contender. (*Earnestly.*) Dad, I know what I'm doing and it always stays within the law . . . just.

PAUL I'm pleased to hear it. It's a long family tradition, playing by the rules . . . that's why we've always been broke! Take your grandfather. He never touched anything unless it had at least three official rubber stamps on it.

AL (*pointing to the plaque*) You should have got his plaque stamped then.

PAUL He'd have liked that . . . given it an air of importance. (*Reading from the plaque as he gives it a final polish.*) "In memory of Albert Burton. 1914 to 1985. Lest they forget".

AL (*now doing a particularly violent loosening up exercise*) If I dropped dead tomorrow would you buy *me* a bench?

PAUL If? If you keep that up it's a racing certainty!

AL	Would you though?

PAUL   It's just a nice practical way of remembering people, that's all . . . I'm not sure I'd want to remember *you*!

AL   I still don't think you should have put Gramps out here on the cliff top, in the middle of nowhere. At least Gran's in the high street . . . even if she is outside that tacky knitwear shop!

PAUL   But that's where she belongs. (*Rising.*) She used to think that shop was marvellous. They always had a fine selection of bargain seconds . . . one sleeve longer than the other, that sort of thing. I spent my whole childhood doing involuntary impersonations of Quasimodo. No, everybody's got a place . . . a place where you especially remember them. That's her place, this is your grandad's. Anyway, I'm not sure your grandma would want to be parked next to him for eternity!

AL   (*sitting on the bench*) Dad, that's rotten!

PAUL   Realistic though. Eternity's a hell of a long time. She used to get sick of him after half an hour. It's sad really . . . as a partner she loved him faithfully; it's just that as a person she couldn't stand the sight of him.

AL   He wasn't that bad!

PAUL   No, but you know what he was like. He used to love it up here. I can just picture him, strutting about, jacket and tie. I don't think I ever saw him without a tie. He used to reckon I was scruffy.

AL   (*tongue in cheek*) He had a point.

PAUL   What!

AL   Well, not scruffy maybe but . . . a bit behind
            the rest of the world . . . a bit sixties-ish.

PAUL   (*astounded*) About what?

AL   (*counting out on his fingers*) Music . . . clothes
            . . . TV programmes . . . films. Do you want
            me to go on?

PAUL   I know what I like.

AL   I know it's difficult when you're old, but you
            could move with the times a bit. Live
            dangerously . . . sell your slide rule and buy a
            calculator!

PAUL   Why don't you just replace me with a micro-
            chip! Anyway, I'm not that old.

AL   Yes you are. I bet you can remember when
            Cliff Richard was just starting out.

PAUL   As it happens I'm much younger than him.

AL   But look at the state of you. If you looked
            like him you'd be fine. You look worse than
            Keith Richard!

PAUL   I've had a hard life.

AL   All I'm saying is you could make a bit of an
            effort. Clothes . . . get a new suit. You know
            I'm trying hard to build the business up. It's
            embarrassing when I have to introduce you.

PAUL   But it's my business!

AL   (*rising*) It's image, dad . . . we need to project
            an image.

PAUL   Yes?

AL   Flared trousers and huge lapels are not the
            image we need. They make you look like a
            grounded hang-glider. We're in the computer
            age now, dad.

PAUL   Computers! Bits and bytes and random this
            and that . . . you just make it up as you go
            along.

            (*A mobile telephone rings inside the sports
            bag.* PAUL *takes it out.*)

            And this bloody thing of yours! You'll be
            wanting me to carry one of these round in my
            new suit pocket I suppose. (*Sitting, he lifts
            the telephone to his ear, but has it the wrong
            way round.*) Hallo.

            (AL *casually reaches over, turns the phone
            round the right way and pulls the aerial up.*
            PAUL *scowls at him.*)

            Hallo . . . it's for you.

            (PAUL *offers the phone to* AL.)

AL   Who is it?

PAUL   I don't know.

AL   Well, could you find out. It's hardly
            professional is it!

PAUL   (*sighing heavily and then adopting his best
            telephone voice*) Excuse me, I wonder if I
            might enquire who is speaking . . . thank you
            so much. If you would be so kind as to hold, I
            will ascertain whether the young Mr Burton is
            available for incoming telephonic
            communication. Thank you.

            (*During the following conversation,* PAUL
            *tries to keep up a constant humming of a
            popular song down the phone.*)

            Are you available then?

AL   Of course I'm available! What are you doing?

PAUL	I've put him on hold. It's one of those songs people put on to make you forget why you've rung up.
AL	Just give it to me, dad. Who is it?
PAUL	Umm . . . I've forgotten now. Mister Somebody from Somewhere and Co.
AL	(*taking the phone in disbelief*) It might be important! (*Into the phone.*) Good afternoon, can I help you?

(PAUL *starts to make himself comfortable on the bench, taking his shoes off and taking a rug out of the bag.*)

. . . Yes, sorry, who's speaking? . . . ah, Mr Gill, yes, I've been expecting you. I know, I'm sorry about that. (*Scowling at* PAUL.) He's new. Care in the community . . . we try to do our bit. (*Listening intently for a moment.*) That sounds fine, perhaps I could fax the info through . . . definitely today, yes . . . right, I'll get that through to you. Bye for now . . . bye.

(AL *hands the phone back to* PAUL.)

(*acidly*) Well done, dad! That was one of the distributors I've been working on for months. You nearly buggered the whole thing up!

PAUL	(*tugging his forelock*) I'm terribly sorry, sir. It won't happen again, sir. Would you like your coffee now, sir?
AL	(*angry*) Get a grip, dad, I'm serious! You might have lost interest in the business but I haven't. I'm going back to send this stuff through.
PAUL	It's Saturday!

AL   The whole business world doesn't stop
            because it's Saturday, only you. In fact these
            days you hardly get going at all.

            (AL *goes towards the stile and then turns back
            to* PAUL.)

            I'm sorry, dad, I know you've been down
            since mum . . . but we've got to carry on
            haven't we?

PAUL   Yeah, I'm sorry. I promise to try and behave
            like a proper grown-up businessman in
            future. Here, I'll come and help you.

AL   No, it's okay. You just stay here and chill out.
            Are you alright?

PAUL   Course I am. You get off.

AL   Right . . . see you.

            (AL *exits over the fence.*)

PAUL   (*talking to the plaque on the bench*) I think
            Al's got about the same confidence in my
            abilities as you had. Maybe you're both right.

            (PAUL *lies down on the bench, using the rug
            as a pillow while the lights dim and music
            from the 1990s plays. The lights rise. About
            one hour has elapsed and* PAUL *is stretched
            out on the bench asleep with a newspaper
            covering his face. His shoes and the telephone
            are together on the ground at the front of the
            bench.* JULIE *stands to one side looking at an
            unfolded map. She is in her mid-twenties,
            well-but-casually dressed, and very
            attractive. The telephone rings and* PAUL, *still
            half asleep, reaches out for it with the paper
            still over his face. He mistakenly grabs a shoe
            and holds it to his ear, watched in amusement
            by* JULIE.)

PAUL	Yeah . . . (*Realizing his mistake, he finally grabs the phone.*) Hello . . . oh, Al, yeah . . . I'm sorry, I'll try to be a bit more efficient next time! . . . no, I wasn't asleep, I was sat here thinking up cunning business strategies . . . it's in the top drawer of my desk . . . maybe I put it somewhere else then . . . I'll be back soon anyway, I'll find it for you . . . yeah, see you soon then, bye.

(PAUL *groans, and eventually sits up. He notices* JULIE *for the first time.* JULIE *is now looking at the map again, with her face turned away from* PAUL.)

	I'm sorry . . . hope this contraption didn't disturb you.
JULIE	(*turning to face* PAUL) It's all right.

(*As* JULIE *turns,* PAUL, *who is still half asleep, looks at her in amazement. His expression changes to one of uncertain recognition and confusion.*)

PAUL	(*softly, half to himself*) Anne!
JULIE	Pardon?
PAUL	(*waking fully*) Sorry! You reminded me . . . bit dazed. I was lost for a second.
JULIE	(*looking at the map again*) I know how you feel.
PAUL	(*putting the phone down*) I don't know why they invented these things. At least when they were on a piece of wire they couldn't follow you about!
JULIE	(*laughing*) More effective than shoes though.
PAUL	(*embarrassed*) Oh, you saw that? I was rather hoping you hadn't.
JULIE	They seem to be getting quite fashionable.

PAUL   (*picking up one of his shoes*) Do you think so?
              My son doesn't. He's threatened to have them
              put down!

JULIE   I meant mobile phones actually.

PAUL   Oh, *you* think the shoes are awful as well.
              They've lasted very well though. They've
              been in and out of fashion four times since I
              got them.

JULIE   You never know your luck. Maybe they'll
              come back again.

PAUL   (*starting to put a shoe on*) Maybe.

JULIE   I know it's unkind to laugh, but there's an old
              man in the town where I live. I think he's a
              bit of a wino actually. He wanders round the
              middle of town talking into his shoe!

PAUL   Maybe he's got a friend with a compatible
              shoe. A well-heeled soul mate.

JULIE   (*laughing*) I'd never thought of that.

PAUL   (*offering one of his shoes*) Give him a ring
              and ask if you like.

JULIE   I think he's on a more modern system.
              (*Looking at the map again.*) Could you tell me
              where I am?

PAUL   I'll try. (*Hopping over to* JULIE, *one shoe on
              and the other in his hand.*) Where do you
              want to be?

JULIE   I'm trying to find my way back to the caravan
              site . . . Beach View.

PAUL   In that case you don't need the map . . . it's
              only a couple of hundred yards up the path.

JULIE   But I've just come past there . . . I didn't see
                 it!

PAUL   Ah well, it's over the other side of a hedge.
                 Beach View's a bit of a misnomer. "Hedge
                 View" would be more accurate.

JULIE   (*starting, very unsuccessfully, to fold the
                 map*) Thanks, I'd have ended up miles away if
                 I hadn't seen you. We only arrived yesterday.

                 (PAUL *sees that* JULIE *is having trouble with
                 the map.*)

PAUL   Here, let me. (*Taking the map from* JULIE.)
                 There's a definite knack to these.

                 (*During the following conversation,* PAUL
                 *tries to fold the map. He is even more inept
                 than* JULIE. *Struggling with the map, the shoe
                 in his hand gets in his way and, without
                 thinking, he passes it to* JULIE *who holds it
                 rather dubiously between thumb and finger.*)

JULIE   I hope you don't think I'm intruding, but
                 when you saw me . . . when you were still
                 half asleep . . . you seemed to think you knew
                 me.

PAUL   I was a bit disorientated. A fairly natural
                 condition for me as it happens. It was just
                 your face, it reminded me . . . somebody I
                 knew a long time ago.

JULIE   But you called me Anne, it just seemed a
                 coincidence.

PAUL   Why, is that what you're called . . . Anne?

JULIE   No, I'm Julie.

PAUL   Oh. Not all that much of a coincidence then.

JULIE	My mother's called Anne though. You looked pleased to see me . . . her . . . Anne. I'm sorry, it's not my business.
PAUL	Don't worry about it.
JULIE	For a second I almost felt guilty.
PAUL	How do you mean?
JULIE	Guilty that I wasn't the person you wanted. You looked so happy and so sad all at the same time.
PAUL	Like I said . . . it's a long time ago. (*Handing the map back to* JULIE *and retrieving his shoe.*) There you go.
	(JULIE *looks at the map which is now more screwed up than folded and in rather a poor condition.*)
JULIE	Great! A knack you said?
PAUL	Yes. I didn't claim I'd got it though. Here, before you go.
	(PAUL *pulls a wallet out of his back pocket.*)
	I'll show you why I got confused.
JULIE	There's no need, honestly . . . I didn't mean to intrude.
	(PAUL *pulls an old and fairly ragged photograph out of the wallet.*)
PAUL	No, but you'll be interested. Sorry about the state of it but it's been in there a long time.
	(JULIE *takes the photograph from* PAUL *and looks at it closely. After a few seconds she looks at* PAUL *in amazement.*)
JULIE	Where did you get this?

PAUL	See what I mean? The hair's different and everything but . . .
JULIE	I don't believe it! Why are you carrying it around?
PAUL	It's just an old friend, that's all. Just a photograph.
JULIE	Just a photograph! But why carry it around in your wallet?
PAUL	Nostalgia, safe keeping, it's not that extraordinary. A lot of people carry photos around with them.
JULIE	Yes, they do. But not of my mother!
PAUL	What!
JULIE	It's my mother. A long time ago, yes, but it's her.
PAUL	(*shocked, in disbelief*) Are you sure?
JULIE	It's her. What's your name?
PAUL	Paul . . . Paul Burton.
JULIE	Paul Burton. I don't remember the name, she hasn't mentioned you.
PAUL	(*rather disappointed*) Hasn't she?
JULIE	This was in her way out, hippy days.
PAUL	Yeah, she was a bit. (*Urgent.*) But how is she, where is she? Maybe you could give me an address or something, I'll write to her.
JULIE	I don't think there's much point in that.
PAUL	What! You've got to tell me . . . what harm would it do? I'm not funny or anything like that.

JULIE   I didn't say you were. I just said there's no
         point in writing. Why not meet her instead?
         She'll be in the caravan.

PAUL   You mean she's here? This is incredible!

JULIE   Come on.

PAUL   I never thought I'd ever see her again! It's
         amazing . . . after all these years. What if she
         doesn't want to see me though . . . it might be
         difficult. What about your father?

JULIE   Mum's on her own, it's all right.

PAUL   No. I'd better not. She probably wouldn't
         remember me. You said she'd never even
         mentioned me. Look, I'll wait here. Would
         you go back and tell her? If she wants to see
         me I'll wait . . . if she doesn't I'll understand.
         Maybe you could come back and tell me.

JULIE   (*shrugging*) If you like, okay. Paul Burton you
         said?

PAUL   That's right.

JULIE   I'll go and tell her then. See you soon. Thanks
         for doing the map.

         (JULIE *turns to exit.*)

PAUL   Julie.

         (JULIE *stops and turns.*)

         Make her come.

JULIE   I'll see what I can do.

         (JULIE *exits stage left as the lights fade and
         music of the 1990s plays. The lights rise and
         the music fades. It is fifteen minutes later and
         PAUL sits on the bench nervously fiddling with
         his hands. He is so engrossed in his thoughts
         that he does not see ANNE enter stage left. She
         is in her late forties, attractive, and*

immaculately groomed. She is just as nervous as PAUL. *She pauses for a moment, watching him, as though in two minds whether to speak or run.*)

ANNE   (*softly*) Paul.

(PAUL *turns, sees her, and stands slowly. There is an awkwardness in the way they react to each other.* PAUL *looks at* ANNE *for a few seconds, shaking his head in disbelief. Unable to find the appropriate words he simply smiles.*)

You're looking well!

(ANNE *approaches* PAUL.)

PAUL   So are you. You're looking fabulous.

(*They stand for a moment, uncertain whether to embrace or shake hands. Eventually* PAUL *takes the initiative and holds out his hand to* ANNE *who holds it for a few seconds rather than shaking it.*)

How have you been?

ANNE   Fine. You?

PAUL   Yeah, just fine. Your dress sense has changed a bit since the last time.

ANNE   (*joking*) Yours hasn't! Julie said you were here. Sorry, that's stupid . . . you know that. I think she's quite phased by the whole thing . . . bumping into someone I knew so long ago.

PAUL   She's not the only one. She's a nice girl.

(*There is an awkward pause.*)

PAUL }   She said that . . .
ANNE   How did you . . .

ANNE   Sorry. You first.

PAUL   She said that you were here on your own, so I
        thought it would be alright to say hallo.

ANNE   Alright?

PAUL   I didn't want to put you in an awkward
        position. If you'd been here with your
        husband or something.

ANNE   I'm not married . . . never got round to it. A
        few near misses but I came out the other side
        unscathed. You?

PAUL   Yes, I got married. I've got a son.

ANNE   Maureen?

PAUL   No . . . we called him Al. We thought
        Maureen might give him an identity crisis.

        (*They both laugh which helps to break the
        ice.*)

ANNE   I mean you married Maureen.

PAUL   Yes I did. In the end it just seemed to work
        out that way.

ANNE   I knew all along that you would. You still live
        around here then?

PAUL   Me and Al, yes. Maureen died last year.

ANNE   I'm sorry.

PAUL   (*sad but without bitterness*) She'd been ill for
        a long time . . . in and out of hospital. The
        last few years weren't that easy for her. I used
        to think it sounded so glib when people called
        death a release . . . now I think I know what
        they mean. So, what are you doing around
        here?

ANNE   Just a break, that's all. Julie's at college and I
        always seem to be so busy with work that we

don't see too much of each other. We actually managed to arrange a few days when we were both free.

PAUL   That's nice. I wish I could say the same about Al and me. We get totally sick of the sight of each other. He's in the business with me . . . no, that's not entirely true. He thinks I'm in the business with him as a kind of junior incompetent partner.

ANNE   Your father . . . did he . . . ?

PAUL   (*smiling*) No. He stuck around for quite a long time making my life hell and enjoying it all tremendously. He's still with us in spirit . . . (*Pointing to the bench.*) Keeping an eye on things.

                (ANNE *goes to the bench and looks at the plaque.*)

ANNE   I always felt so guilty.

PAUL   There was no need. In the end we practically had to shoot him. So, what do you do now, you mentioned work?

ANNE   Fashion design. I spent a year or two wandering around, here and there, then realized I wasn't actually going anywhere. I had Julie and decided that I really needed to be earning some money.

PAUL   Al's trying to put me into semi-retirement, encouraging me to play golf, but I'm hopeless. My putter's still in its wrapper . . . never got a ball on the green yet. How long are you here for?

ANNE   A few days, then I've got some business meetings in London. I'm hoping to get back here for a while afterwards. Julie's here for a couple of weeks with her friend.

> (*The telephone rings inside the bag.* ANNE
> *looks at it in surprise.*)

ANNE   Your bag's ringing.

PAUL   It's one of BT's new-style phone boxes.

ANNE   Shouldn't you answer it?

PAUL   No, it might be for me, it's bound to be
          unpleasant! Nobody ever rings me with good
          news. (*Remembering.*) Oh, hell! I was
          supposed to be going back to the office to get
          something for Al. (*Taking the phone out of
          the bag.*) Here, you answer it.

ANNE   Me!

PAUL   Yes, that'll fox him. Tell him you're . . . tell
          him you're the China Palace take-away . . .
          he's always ringing them.

ANNE   I can't.

PAUL   (*handing* ANNE *the phone*) Course you can.
          Serve him right for pestering me. China
          Palace.

ANNE   (*into the phone, trying hard at a Chinese
          accent between fits of giggles*) Harro, China
          Parace . . . no, velly solly. This is China
          Parace Lestaulant . . . Velly good, no
          probrem. Hokay.

          (ANNE *gives the phone back to* PAUL *and
          dissolves into fits of laughter. In doing so she
          clings onto* PAUL *for support.*)

PAUL   Well?

ANNE   He sounded a bit confused at first. Then he
          pulled himself together, said "what the hell"
          and ordered a special chow mein to pick up in
          half an hour!

PAUL	Just one? You mean he didn't order me anything? The sneaky bugger!
	(*They both realize that they are holding each other and break away, slightly embarrassed.*)
ANNE	He sounded very efficient, when he'd got over the initial shock.
PAUL	Oh, he'll be busy now reprogramming all the stored numbers. He'll be devastated he got a wrong one.
ANNE	He'll be even more devastated when he gets to the Chinese and his noodles aren't cooked.
PAUL	God, I hadn't thought of that. Poor devils . . . he'll give them his incompetence speech! I'd call him back if I could ever remember what our office number was. (*Reluctantly.*) Look, I'm sorry but I'll have to get back. I promised to find something for him . . . something I've apparently lost!
ANNE	That's okay.
PAUL	Normally it wouldn't matter but we had a few words earlier . . . I'd better show willing. (*Collecting his things together.*) It's good seeing you again.
ANNE	Yes.
PAUL	Look, seeing as Al's decided I'm old enough to feed myself, could we have a meal together or something? (*Hurriedly.*) If you'd rather not, I'd understand.
ANNE	I'd like to. I'd like to very much. I think Julie and her friend would be more than pleased to get me out of the way. I'm something of a dark cloud hanging over their social activities.
PAUL	Tonight then? Seven o'clock?

ANNE	I'll look forward to it.
PAUL	I'll pick you up at the site entrance.
ANNE	I'll be there. I'm vegetarian, does that cause any problem?
PAUL	(*climbing over the stile*) None whatsoever, I was only intending buying you a bag of chips anyway! See you later.
ANNE	Paul?
PAUL	Yeah?
ANNE	(*hesitant*) You didn't say anything to Julie did you, about how we met?
PAUL	No, I don't think so. Why, are you ashamed of me?
ANNE	(*relieved*) No, of course not! It's just that I try to play those days down a bit. I don't want Julie to develop all the wild ideas I used to think were so great.
PAUL	If I see her again I'll just be vague . . . it comes naturally anyway. See you later.
	(PAUL *exits, leaving* ANNE *reflecting on the meeting. She sits on the bench as* JULIE *enters from stage left.*)
JULIE	That was quick!
ANNE	He had to go . . . we're meeting up again later. I thought you were staying back at the caravan?
JULIE	(*nonchalantly*) Oh, I just thought I'd take a walk.
ANNE	And see what I was up to! How long have you been lurking?

JULIE	Just a minute or two.
ANNE	It's mothers who are supposed to keep an eye on their daughters, not the other way round.
JULIE	I was worried about you . . . coming here on your own, talking to a strange man.
ANNE	You were here on your own with him!
JULIE	That's different.
ANNE	And why is that different! You ought to be more careful.
JULIE	He hasn't been wandering around for the last God knows how long with a photograph of me in his pocket. That's weird. Did you find out why?
ANNE	No, not yet. Maybe he doesn't always carry it around. It might just be a coincidence.
JULIE	Some coincidence! I think he always has it with him. How do you know each other?
ANNE	We really didn't know each other all that well.
JULIE	Come on . . . tell me all about it.
ANNE	There's nothing to tell.
JULIE	But I want to know . . . how, why, when?
ANNE	(*evasive*) I can't remember . . . a party I think it was . . . friend of a friend.
JULIE	(*disappointed*) That's all?
ANNE	That's all. There was nothing to it.
JULIE	But if there was nothing to it, then the photograph is even stranger. Do you think he's sick or something?

ANNE   Maybe he was just stunned by my beauty.

JULIE   (*teasing*) Nobody could be that sick!
            (*Dramatic.*) Maybe he's been madly and
            passionately in love with you for all these
            years, pining for the day you'd return to set
            his soul free!

ANNE   Who's being sick now! Shouldn't you be
            getting ready for your night out?

JULIE   I suppose so. When are you seeing lover boy?

ANNE   I'm seeing Paul tonight, so you and Sam are
            on your own. You don't mind do you?

JULIE   We'll survive somehow. Are you coming?

ANNE   You go on ahead. I'll sit here for awhile. I
            won't be long.

JULIE   Okay. Here, I've still got his photograph.
            You'd better give it back. (*Glancing at the
            photograph as she hands it to* ANNE.) You
            look really weird!

ANNE   Thanks very much.

JULIE   Just a friend of a friend?

ANNE   Sorry.

JULIE   What a disappointment!

            (JULIE *exits.*)

ANNE   (*to herself as she looks at the photograph*)
            Friend of a friend? Not quite, no.

            (*The lights fade. Music of the late 1960s
            plays, setting the period for the following
            scene.*)

                        Scene Two

*The summer of 1969. It is the same section of the cliff top,
but there is no bench and an older signpost indicates the way*

to Freshwater. ALBERT *clambers over the stile and stands centre stage surveying the view out to sea. He is in his late fifties, wears spectacles, and is dressed in flannels, sports jacket and tie. He regards himself as a self-made man and is rather pompous and overbearing. Music fades.*

ALBERT   Right, this'll do us. Just look at that view eh? Just take a look at that. (*He glances round and, realizing that he is on his own, shouts back over the fence.*) Come on, get a move on.

(ALBERT *shakes his head in disbelief as* OLIVE *and* PAUL *enter over the stile.* OLIVE, *his wife, is in her mid-fifties and wears a home-made dress and thick cardigan. She is carrying a large handbag and a bag containing a flask and plastic cups.* PAUL *is in his early twenties and is dressed in jeans and open-necked shirt. He brings up the rear struggling under the weight of two deck chairs, a rug and a large bag containing packs of sandwiches and cake.*)

Come on, help your mother.

(PAUL *tries to help* OLIVE *who gets her foot stuck in the stile and is stranded halfway over.*)

OLIVE   Ooh, don't push, I'm loosing my shoe.

ALBERT   (*looking on without offering to help*) This side . . . you want to get this side of her, you'll never shift her like that. You need some leverage. God help us, what do you think this is, a picnic!

(PAUL *reluctantly dumps his load over the fence and climbs over to help* OLIVE.)

PAUL   You mean I've carried this food all the way here and it's not a picnic?

ALBERT   'Ey, less lip. Just get your mother down off
                there. She looks like a fairy up a Christmas
                tree. Take her weight, go on take her weight.

                (PAUL *gives a final pull and manages to free*
                OLIVE.)

OLIVE   (*struggling down*) It's always the same with
                your father, it always turns into a route
                march! (*Examining her dress.*) I've snagged
                my frock now!

ALBERT   (*admiring the view again*) You don't want to
                worry about that. Just look at that view. Best
                view on the island that is. Fit for a king.

                (PAUL *slowly picks up the chairs and bag.*)

OLIVE   He knows I can't walk as fast as him. I can't
                walk like you, Albert. I don't know why I
                bother coming with him, he's always fifty
                yards in front. One of my best frocks this!

PAUL   Come on, mum, his majesty's not listening.

                (PAUL *crosses behind* ALBERT *and is about to
                continue the walk.*)

ALBERT   Where are you off to now! This'll do here . . .
                we always stop here.

OLIVE   I wouldn't mind a change now and again. I
                think it's better the other way.

ALBERT   Don't start that again, Olive. You know you
                like it best this way, just take my word for it.
                You get the view this way. Let's have these
                chairs up then.

PAUL   We're not staying up here are we? I thought
                we'd be going down onto the beach.

ALBERT   Just get them up. It's no use going down
                    there, you don't get the view. Anyway, your
                    mother would get sand in her stockings.

                    (PAUL *reluctantly puts the deck chairs up.*)

PAUL   She could always take them off. I mean, I
                    know it's never happened before, but she
                    could take them off. What do you think, mum,
                    is the world ready for it?

OLIVE   Paul, get away with you!

ALBERT   Your mother's not getting undressed up here,
                    not in broad daylight! Anyway, how would we
                    get her down there? We'd need a block and
                    tackle. Just have some consideration.

PAUL   We might just as well have stopped in the
                    back garden. Better still, we could have sat in
                    the car on the drive . . . nice and warm, save
                    petrol!

OLIVE   (*sitting in the first deck chair*) I wouldn't
                    mind going on the beach occasionally. It'd
                    make a change. You get the wind up here.

ALBERT   Just the job . . . get the cobwebs out of your
                    hair. (*To* PAUL.) It'll do you good to get some
                    fresh air inside you instead of sitting inside
                    listening to all that rubbish of yours!

PAUL   It isn't rubbish, dad, it's music. Just because
                    you don't understand it!

ALBERT   Understand it? I can't see how anybody can
                    understand it! It sounds like a bunch of
                    wailing cats. If that's music I'm a Dutchman!

PAUL   Go and stick your finger in a dyke then.

OLIVE   Paul, you shouldn't speak to your father like
                    that.

PAUL   Well, he asks for it. Just because it's different
                to what you had in your day doesn't
                necessarily make it bad.

ALBERT   (*sitting*) I'll say it's different. We used to like
                to know what people were singing about. Pass
                me the paper, Olive.

OLIVE   (*searching in the bags*) That Russ what's-his-
                name, I don't mind him. You don't hear much
                of him now though do you?

ALBERT   Vera Lynn. Now there's a singer for you.
                Kept us going, I'll tell you, in the forces. I
                remember once, 1943 it was, me and Knocker
                Northfield had just . . .

PAUL   Not the war, dad . . . not again!

ALBERT   And what's wrong with the war! I'll tell you
                what my lad, it was the making of my
                generation. We didn't have time to wander
                about with hair round our ankles listening to
                the rubbish you listen to. Britain's finest hour
                that was . . .

                (PAUL *mouths the remainder of the speech.*)

                . . . made men of us, those of us who came
                through it.

PAUL   But we don't have to live in the past do we?
                Why can't you understand that we're just a
                different generation? We've got different
                values to you.

ALBERT   Lest we forget, eh? It's a bloody good job
                some of us remember, that's all I can say.

PAUL   I'm not saying we should forget. I'm just
                saying that things are different now. You
                expect us to understand you, but you never
                make any effort to understand us. I know it's
                a strange concept but personally I've no

particular desire to travel the world blowing it up as I go along . . . sorry.

ALBERT Aye, well, maybe that's what's wrong with you.

OLIVE (*with a sudden flash of inspiration*) Side Saddle.

(ALBERT *looks at* OLIVE *quizzically*.)

That's one of his records, Side Saddle.

ALBERT One of whose records?

OLIVE Russ what's-his-name. I liked that one.

ALBERT (*in despair*) Russ what's-his-name! Have you found that paper yet?

OLIVE (*passing a newspaper to* ALBERT) I think it was Side Saddle . . . they all sound a bit similar. Still, it can't be easy with a finger missing.

(ALBERT *and* PAUL *both look at* OLIVE *in total disbelief. Then there is a moment's pause as* ALBERT *starts to read his paper,* OLIVE *struggles with her memory and* PAUL *sits on the grass looking rather moodily out to sea*.)

It's nice to have you with us for a change, Paul. You never seem to do anything with us these days.

ALBERT Too busy listening to his records, that's why.

OLIVE We used to do all sorts . . . do you remember, when you were small? All sorts we used to do.

ALBERT No time for us now though has he. That's the trouble with his generation, no family values. Too busy with their records and their cannabis resin. (*Which he pronounces cannarbis raisin*.)

PAUL   But I thought that was the whole point . . .
            you bring children up so that they can go out
            into the big bad world and mess up their own
            lives!

ALBERT   But at least we had time for our parents . . .
            when we didn't have a war to fight. In fact we
            had to fight wars for our parents . . . and our
            children.

PAUL   And our children's children.

ALBERT   You're happy enough to rely on me when it
            comes to work though aren't you? You don't
            mind having your nose in the business . . .
            we're good enough for you then.

PAUL   I didn't say you weren't good enough. I just
            like to have a little time to myself.

OLIVE   Lovely little lad you were. Never a minute's
            trouble was he, Albert?

ALBERT   He's making up for it now though!

PAUL   Dad, I'm twenty-one! I can change my own
            nappy!

ALBERT   Twenty-one! Do you know where I was when
            I was twenty-one? Fighting for King and
            country.

OLIVE   You were in Cleckheaton.

ALBERT   Who was?

OLIVE   The war hadn't started then. You were still
            living in Cleckheaton with your mother.

ALBERT   Olive, does it matter! I was just speaking
            figuratively!

OLIVE   Well, I'm just saying you were in
            Cleckheaton. In fact even when the war got

started you were still in Cleckheaton most of the time . . . with your bad feet.

ALBERT Look, I couldn't help my feet could I? I'm just saying that he'll have to change his ways soon. When he gets married . . . that'll waken him up.

PAUL Why should getting married change me?

OLIVE It changed your father! Very pleasant he was until we got married. You ought to be getting yourself a bit more organized though. Four weeks, that's all you've got. Have you got your suit ordered yet?

PAUL There's plenty of time, mum.

OLIVE It's a pity your Maureen couldn't come with us today.

PAUL She was busy. Bridesmaids' dresses or something.

OLIVE Well, I'm pleased to see she's organized. You ought to get your suit ordered, it'll be too late.

PAUL I'll have to wear jeans then.

OLIVE Paul!

PAUL Just a joke . . . a little joke.

OLIVE It's no good leaving things to the last minute, Paul. Rome wasn't built in a day.

PAUL I'm sure they could've knocked up a toga in a month though! Don't worry.

OLIVE Well, somebody's got to! Lovely girl she is. You'll have to get your hair cut as well.

PAUL What for?

OLIVE

What for! You can't be getting married looking like that! Maureen'll be making an effort, so the least you can do is have a decent haircut. You could go with your dad. Every fortnight your dad goes. I'll book you in . . . then you won't be waiting. What do you think, Albert?

ALBERT

(*engrossed in his newspaper*) Mmm.

OLIVE

Course, if they don't do bookings you'll just have to wait. Have you thought about buttonholes?

PAUL

Oh, constantly . . . I could hardly get to sleep last night!

OLIVE

Paul! There's no need for that. Somebody's got to think ahead.

PAUL

Mum, can't you just give it a rest? Why does everybody try to organize my life for me? If it's not you it's dad, or Maureen, or her mum.

OLIVE

We're only doing what's best.

PAUL

What's best for you or for me? Why can't you all just leave me alone!

OLIVE

Oh, so it's come to that now has it? After all we've done for you! Did you hear that, Albert?

PAUL

I didn't mean it like that.

OLIVE

Scrimped and saved we have . . . to make things nice for you. Always had a holiday, always had nice toys. And that's the thanks we get.

PAUL

I'm not saying . . .

OLIVE

It's all right, Paul, there's no need to make excuses. I just wish I'd known, that's all.

(*Sniffing into a handkerchief.*) Still, we know now. We know what you think of us now.

(*There is an uneasy silence for several seconds.*)

PAUL   (*reluctantly, knowing that victory is impossible*) I'll get the suit ordered tomorrow.

OLIVE   No, it's all right, you please yourself, Paul. I know when I'm not wanted. You just get on with it. I was only trying to help.

PAUL   Look, I'm sorry, I just got annoyed, all right? You can come with me if you like.

OLIVE   I wouldn't want to interfere. That's the last thing I've ever wanted to do.

PAUL   I'm asking you. Come with me.

OLIVE   Well, all right, if that's what you want. You'll need some shoes as well.

PAUL   Without a doubt.

OLIVE   I saw some nice smart ones the other day . . . lace up. You don't want those slip-on ones, they never look nice.

ALBERT   Bloody hell, it's on again!

OLIVE   Albert, not in front of Paul!

ALBERT   I thought we'd seen the end of it last year. All over the place they'll be . . . like a bloody rash!

OLIVE   Who will?

ALBERT   This pop festival rubbish. It's on again this week. Took over the place last year. Everywhere you look for miles around they'll be wandering about in a bloody daze . . . the great unwashed. You'd have thought the Council would have put a stop to it.

OLIVE   I don't remember.

ALBERT   You must do! Thousands of them there were
            . . . like a plague of Afghan Hounds. Not a
            bar of soap between 'em.

OLIVE   Oh yes, I'm with you now. Some of them
            were a bit funny weren't they? At least our
            Paul's not like that.

ALBERT   I'll tell you what, that'd be the day, that'd be
            the day eh! When a son of mine wandered
            round like that. A dose of National Service,
            that's what they need.

PAUL   It's only a music festival! Even young people
            have got a right to enjoy themselves haven't
            they?

ALBERT   Not round here they haven't! Some of us pay
            rates. If I wanted clowns on my doorstep I'd
            run off and join a circus.

OLIVE   You want to keep out of their way, Paul.
            Invite Maureen round, you can finalise
            arrangements.

PAUL   Why should I keep out of their way!

OLIVE   They take drugs.

PAUL   A few of them might, but it's not compulsory.
            Anyway, you take them . . . every week
            you're round at the doctors.

OLIVE   (indignant) Paul, those are not drugs . . .
            those are prescribed medication. The doctor
            says I have to take them because I live with
            your father.

ALBERT   Just look at this lot eh . . . just look at 'em.
            Fat Mattress, Blodwyn Pig. They must be on
            drugs to think their names up! Who's this
            Dylan feller?

OLIVE   Oh, I like him. I didn't realize he sang. Under
                Milk Wood, I liked that one.

ALBERT   Not him, he's dead! This Dylan bloke in the
                paper . . . he's one of the star turns.

PAUL   He's only one of the greatest turns ever . . .
                after Vera Lynn of course! He's the new
                forces' sweetheart.

ALBERT   'Ey, don't you go taking her name in vain.
                It's very likely we'd have lost the war without
                her. (*Fondly.*) Brought comfort and succour to
                the forces she did.

PAUL   I thought the NAAFI did that!

ALBERT   What do you mean the NAAFI? She wasn't in
                the NAAFI!

PAUL   Why was she bringing supper then?

ALBERT   I didn't say supper . . .

OLIVE   Albert, take no notice of him. He's only
                trying to get you going.

ALBERT   No respect, that's his trouble. At least I had
                some respect for my father. I had respect for
                his belt, I know that. A very hard man my
                father was . . . hard but fair. He always told
                you why he was thrashing you. Are we eating
                those sandwiches then?

OLIVE   Do you want them now? I thought it was a bit
                early.

ALBERT   Course I want them now. If we leave them
                much longer we'll be taking them back home
                with us.

OLIVE   (*rummaging in the bags*) I thought you'd want
                to leave it a bit. We can eat now if you like.
                Do you want your pullover, Paul?

PAUL   I'd rather have cheese.

OLIVE	It's here when you want it. You don't want to go catching a cold. That's the last thing you want on your wedding day. (*To* ALBERT.) Potted meat or tuna?
ALBERT	Tuna! Is that all there is?
OLIVE	There's potted meat. It's all I'd got in. If I'd known I'd have got something in. Paul?
PAUL	No thanks.
OLIVE	Come on, you need to get something inside you. You'll be wasting away.
PAUL	I'm all right. I'm not hungry.
OLIVE	You never eat, that's your trouble. It's why you're so moody. Albert?
ALBERT	I'll have potted meat then, if that's all there is.
OLIVE	There's tuna.
ALBERT	You know I don't like tuna. Foreign rubbish!
OLIVE	What do you mean, foreign rubbish . . . it's fish! You like fish.
ALBERT	I like British fish . . . that's foreign fish. Just give me a potted meat will you! You know where you are with potted meat.
	(OLIVE *passes a packet of sandwiches to* ALBERT *who then munches on one as he gazes out to sea.* OLIVE *pours tea into three plastic cups.*)
OLIVE	I always thought you liked tuna.
	(ANNE *enters, stage left. She is in her early twenties, very attractive, and is dressed in a kaftan. Long hair is held from her face by a headband. She is carrying a collection of shells, wrapped in a scarf. Looking for someone, she wanders across stage to look out over the stile.*)

ALBERT	(*watching in disbelief*) Here they come, look . . . it's starting! Minnie Ha-Ha! Just look at the state of that . . . I'll bet she's on something!
ANNE	(*calling out over the stile*) Shirley . . . Shirley!
ALBERT	Do you mind!
ANNE	(*louder*) Shirley!
ALBERT	I said, do you mind!
ANNE	(*turning*) I'm sorry. Were you speaking to me?
ALBERT	Yes, young lady. I said, do you mind. I'm trying to eat a potted meat sandwich here!
ANNE	I'm sorry, I didn't realize.
ALBERT	No, you wouldn't. If you'd let some air get to your ears you might hear something.
OLIVE	Albert! There's no need to be rude.
ALBERT	I've got a right to speak my mind. That's what we fought the war for. (*To* ANNE.) Just a bit of consideration, young lady, that's all I'm asking.
ANNE	Look, I'm sorry. I'm just trying to find my sister.
ALBERT	Well, you won't find her in my potted meat sandwich. I suggest you look somewhere else.
ANNE	Okay, stay cool!

(ANNE *starts to climb the stile*.)

OLIVE	She's not doing any harm. (*To* ANNE.) Just a minute, love, can I help?
ANNE	It doesn't matter. I can see I'm stirring up bad vibes.

OLIVE   Oh, don't take any notice of my husband,
                 love. He's just a bit liverish. It always affects
                 his . . . what was its?

ANNE   (*amused*) Vibes.

OLIVE   Yes, he's a martyr to them! What does your
                 friend look like?

ANNE   (*not certain how to react*) My twin sister . . .
                 she's taller.

ALBERT   (*to himself*) There's a whole bloody tribe of
                 'em!

ANNE   We're here for the festival.

ALBERT   (*quietly*) We'd never have guessed.

OLIVE   Oh, I'm sorry. We didn't see anybody like
                 you. My husband would have noticed,
                 wouldn't you, Albert?

ANNE   (*warming to* OLIVE) I'm sure she was coming
                 this way. I was down on the beach.

OLIVE   I'd hang on here then, love. The paths go all
                 ways up there, you'll never find her. She's
                 bound to come back for you. Would you like a
                 sandwich while you wait?

                 (*At the mention of sandwiches,* ALBERT
                 *attempts to hold his remaining potted meat
                 ones safely out of sight until he is certain that
                 he won't have to share them.*)

ANNE   No thanks. I'd better look for her.

OLIVE   It's no trouble. Here, sit down and have a cup
                 of tea, you look tired out.

                 (ANNE *notices* PAUL *for the first time. They
                 exchange eye contact and* ANNE *decides to
                 stay.* OLIVE *starts pouring tea into the beaker
                 from the flask.*)

Paul, your tea's here, don't let it go cold. (*To* ANNE.) Sugar?

ANNE   No thanks. You're very kind.

OLIVE   It's all right. My husband was very rude.

ANNE   I don't mind. Lots of old people are. It's the way I dress . . . I've got used to it.

(ALBERT *almost chokes on his sandwich.*)

ALBERT Old! You're saying I'm old now?

ANNE   I'm sorry, I meant older.

ALBERT I'll tell you something, young lady . . .

OLIVE   Not now, Albert!

ALBERT I'm just stating my case here, if you don't mind. I may look old and past it to you, but I'm a respected member of this community. A community that doesn't want your lot here!

ANNE   I'm sorry . . .

ALBERT I bring money into this community. You might have heard of us . . . Burton's Board Games. (*Almost spelling the slogan out with his hands.*) "If you're bored of board games, try Burton's boards", that's me!

OLIVE   Albert, she's not interested in all that.

ALBERT Well, she ought to be.

OLIVE   Anyway, I think it's a very nice frock. Here's your tea, love.

ANNE   (*taking the tea*) Thanks. This is really cool.

OLIVE   I'm sorry, love . . . I need to get a new flask. This one's past it I'm afraid. Paul?

ANNE   No, the tea's fine. (*Offering to take* PAUL'S *tea to him.*) Shall I?

OLIVE	Oh, yes. That's Paul, our little boy.

(PAUL *glares at* OLIVE *in disgust as* ANNE *takes a cup of tea to him. She is trying hard to suppress a giggle.*)

ALBERT	(*to* OLIVE) You should have let her get off. She doesn't want your tea . . . she's one of this festival bunch!
OLIVE	She looks clean enough.
ALBERT	Just keep her off my potted meat, that's all.
OLIVE	(*to* ANNE) Very nice down on the beach round here, isn't it?
ANNE	Yeah, fantastic. I was collecting shells.
OLIVE	Oh. Did you get some nice ones?
ANNE	Yeah, really groovy. Would you like to see?
OLIVE	Oh, yes, lovely.

(ANNE *places the collection of shells on* OLIVE'S *lap.*)

ANNE	They're so natural aren't they? I use them for decorations . . . jewellery.
OLIVE	Mmm, lovely.

(ANNE *returns to sit by* PAUL, *leaving* OLIVE *to examine the shells.*)

Look, Albert, shells.

(ALBERT *grunts.*)

Very natural aren't they?

ALBERT	Course they're natural, they're bloody shells!
OLIVE	Lovely though. Very groovy, look . . . see they're all curly.

PAUL	(*to* ANNE) You don't have to drink that.
ANNE	It's okay, I want to . . . your mother wants me to.
OLIVE	Look at this one, Albert, it's pink.
ANNE	(*to* PAUL) Are you on holiday?
PAUL	No, we live here.
ANNE	Really. Far out.
PAUL	No, just up the road.

(ANNE *looks sharply at* PAUL, *thinking that he is patronizing her, but he gives her a disarming grin.*)

Sorry . . . I've caught it off my mother.

ANNE	(*joining in with the joke*) No, it's my fault. The words kind of go with the outfit. I only do it to live up to people's expectations. I'd love to live somewhere like this.
PAUL	It's okay . . . a bit quiet.
ANNE	But everything's so fresh . . . the air, the sea. It makes you feel as though you're alive, you can breathe.
PAUL	Yeah, well that's about as exciting as it gets. Just don't breathe too loudly or else they'll deport you back to the mainland.
ANNE	We're here for the festival but we decided to come for the whole week . . . try to sell some stuff.
PAUL	(*hopefully*) Stuff!
ANNE	No, stuff we make at the commune. Are you going?

PAUL	No, I don't think so. It's different when you live here.
ANNE	Why? There's still the music . . . the people. That's what it's all about. I get the impression your father doesn't approve.
PAUL	Oh, don't take any notice of him, he's just jealous. He desperately wants to go but my mother won't let him. He's been growing his hair specially for a couple of days now.
ANNE	He should go like that. He'd be the freakiest person there!
PAUL	I'm sure he'd really like that! I'm sorry he went on at you.
ANNE	That's okay, I don't think parents were ever young!
PAUL	My dad wasn't! My grandparents never had children . . . just him!
OLIVE	(*to* ALBERT) I could collect shells if we ever went down on the beach.
ALBERT	Then what would you do with them!
OLIVE	I could decorate things.
ALBERT	(*giving* OLIVE *one of his looks of pure disbelief*) You'll be wandering round with flowers stuck in your rollers soon! Is there any cake in there?
OLIVE	Battenburg.
ALBERT	Battenburg! You know I don't like marzipan.
OLIVE	You can pull it off.
ALBERT	There'll be nothing left!

(OLIVE *unpacks a piece of cake and passes it to* ALBERT *who carefully dissects it, passing each piece of marzipan to* OLIVE.)

PAUL   (*to* ANNE) Actually, I thought about going to the festival but none of my friends are going. Besides, it's not the same, living here . . . going home every night.

ANNE   Don't then . . . don't go home. Crash out with us.

PAUL   What? You wouldn't mind?

ANNE   Why should we? We're all here for the same reason aren't we? Shirley and I share everything.

PAUL   I don't think it would go down very well.

ANNE   With your parents? They don't own you. You're as free as a bird, we all are. They can't dictate who you are and what you do.

PAUL   Oh, it's not just them. (*Reluctantly.*) There's my girlfriend . . . fiancée.

ANNE   So, bring her along.

PAUL   Maureen! She'd hate it. She thinks flower power's all about baking.

ANNE   Okay, so go without her. She doesn't own you either.

PAUL   She thinks she does! (*Worried.*) That's the trouble.

OLIVE   Paul, do you want your father's marzipan?

PAUL   No thanks. (*To* ANNE.) It sticks in his teeth!

OLIVE   What about you, love, piece of cake?

ANNE   No, really.

OLIVE	More tea then?
ANNE	No thanks. I ought to look for my sister. (*To* PAUL *as she rises.*) So, are you coming to the festival?
PAUL	I don't know. Can I walk with you for a while? I'll show you the way.
ANNE	Yeah . . . why not?
OLIVE	Don't forget your shells. Lovely they are.
ANNE	Thanks. Thanks for the tea.

(ANNE *moves to take the shells from* OLIVE.)

OLIVE	That's all right, love. Sorry it was cold. I hope you enjoy your festival.
ANNE	(*with a quick glance at* PAUL) I have a feeling I just might.
OLIVE	You want to be careful though. There're some very funny people about aren't there, Albert? I don't suppose that Russ what's-his-name is on is he? I quite like him.
PAUL	No, mum. I'm just going to show . . . (*Realizing he doesn't know her name.*)
ANNE	Anne.
PAUL	I'm just showing Anne the way.
OLIVE	(*surprised*) Oh, well don't be long. (*Pointedly.*) Your Maureen'll be expecting you. Here, you'd best take your pullover.
PAUL	I'm fine, I don't need it. (*Taking the marzipan from* OLIVE.) I'll be back soon.
OLIVE	I thought you didn't want that.
PAUL	It's for the birds.

(PAUL *leads* ANNE *off, over the stile.*)

ANNE	Bye.

OLIVE   Bye, love. Albert, she's going.

(ALBERT *grunts vaguely in* ANNE's *direction as she exits with* PAUL.)

I don't know what our Paul's thinking of, going off with her like that! Whatever would his Maureen say?

ALBERT   All sorts if I know Maureen. Got her head screwed on has that girl. You shouldn't have encouraged them.

OLIVE   I didn't encourage anybody. I was only being sociable.

ALBERT   Offering her our tea! (*Gazing out to sea.*) Have you seen that lot out there? I've been keeping my eye on them.

OLIVE   Ooh, they're on the rocks!

ALBERT   Well if they don't get off soon they'll be drowning . . . silly beggars!

OLIVE   Somebody should tell them. They're only young girls.

ALBERT   Girls! How do you know they're girls? There'll be all sorts in that lot. Just look at the state of 'em! Can't tell one from another. Hermaphrodites, that's what they are. We've bred a generation of hermaphrodites!

OLIVE   I didn't breed them.

(OLIVE *gazes out to sea while* ALBERT *returns to his newspaper.*)

Albert. They're taking their clothes off!

ALBERT   What!

OLIVE   Going swimming, look.

44

(*They both gaze out to sea for a few seconds.*)

They are girls! I told you. (*Not knowing where to look.*)

ALBERT   You can't tell at this distance.

OLIVE   Yes I can. It's your eyes. Let me have that crossword, I'm not watching them.

(ALBERT *passes the paper over to* OLIVE, *hardly able to take his eyes off the scene in front of him. He reaches into the bag for a pair of binoculars and tries to look out to the beach, but he has problems trying to see through them whilst wearing his spectacles. He finally gives up in frustration.*)

ALBERT   Bloody things! Are you sure?

OLIVE   What about?

ALBERT   Girls.

OLIVE   Of course I'm sure.

(ALBERT *watches for a few more seconds.*)

ALBERT   (*casually*) I'm just going for a stroll.

OLIVE   What?

ALBERT   A stroll. (*Rising.*) I won't be long.

OLIVE   You're not going down there!

ALBERT   Well, somebody's got to . . . somebody's got to warn them. Very dangerous those rocks.

OLIVE   Albert!

ALBERT   Just you get on with your crossword. Leave this to me.

(ALBERT *exits.*)

OLIVE   Albert . . . Albert!

(*The lights fade as music of the 1960s plays.
When the lights come up it is an hour later.
Music fades.* OLIVE *is doing the crossword in
the paper. She glances up, sees something,
and hurriedly looks back to the newspaper.*
PAUL *enters over the stile.*)

PAUL   Hi, mum.

OLIVE   Oh, hallo, love. You've been a long time!

PAUL   Just walking.

OLIVE   Well, it's time we were getting back. I'll have
           to get the tea on for your dad. Not that he
           deserves any!

PAUL   You've eaten. I thought that was the idea of
           bringing the picnic.

OLIVE   Your dad'll still want some tea. Those
           sandwiches won't keep him going. I can't get
           this seven across.

PAUL   Where is he anyway?

OLIVE   Never you mind. He went off for a walk . . .
           just after you went. I come out for a nice
           afternoon and end up sitting here by myself! I
           might just as well have stayed at home. Did
           she find her sister?

PAUL   Eventually. (*Sitting next to* OLIVE.) Mum?

OLIVE   Part of a flower, beginning with 'S'.

PAUL   What?

OLIVE   Part of a flower. You should know this, you
           got your 'O' level.

PAUL   (*cautiously*) I think I'm going away for a few
           days.

OLIVE   Where to?

PAUL   Just away . . . a break. I haven't had a holiday this year.

OLIVE   Yes you have. What about Easter with your dad and me?

PAUL   No, I mean by myself.

OLIVE   What do you mean by yourself? What do you want to be going off by yourself for?

PAUL   Just a break, that's all.

OLIVE   You'll be off on your honeymoon in a few weeks' time.

PAUL   I know.

OLIVE   (*suspicious*) You're not thinking of sneaking off somewhere with Maureen are you?

PAUL   It'll be a pretty boring honeymoon if I don't!

OLIVE   No, now. Because if you are you can think again. It wouldn't be right.

PAUL   The last thing I intend doing is taking Maureen with me.

OLIVE   Your father and I waited. I'm not saying we were perfect but we had proper morals in those days. We knew right from wrong.

PAUL   I'm not going with Maureen.

OLIVE   Not that your father didn't try, but I wouldn't let him. Where are you going?

PAUL   Oh, anywhere, just away. (*Vaguely.*) I might visit Mike in Portsmouth.

OLIVE   And what about Maureen, does she know about this?

PAUL   I'll tell her. She doesn't own me . . . yet!

OLIVE	Well, it seems a queer going on to me. You'll have to tell your father, it might not be convenient.
PAUL	He owes me loads of holiday. He can't really say no.
OLIVE	That's between you and him, don't drag me into it. When are you going?
PAUL	Tomorrow I think.
OLIVE	Tomorrow? Why didn't you say . . . I've got nothing washed!
PAUL	I don't need much.
OLIVE	Well, you'll need clean underwear, what would people think?
PAUL	I promise that I won't go round showing everybody my underwear.
OLIVE	What if you have an accident? I'll have to get them in tonight. They'll never dry. You should have said last week.
PAUL	Don't worry about it, it's all right. (*Looking out to sea.*) Is that dad out there?
OLIVE	(*going back to her crossword*) Probably. Just ignore him.
PAUL	But he keeps waving.
OLIVE	He's been waving for the last half hour.
PAUL	What's he done wrong?
OLIVE	He hasn't done anything wrong!
PAUL	Yes he has, I know you better than that. (*Pause.*) Mum, do you think I'm doing the right thing . . . with Maureen?
OLIVE	How do you mean?

PAUL   I don't know. Up until a few months ago I
              thought it was what I wanted . . . getting
              married. Now it's getting closer I'm not sure
              any more.

OLIVE   It's just nerves, Paul, that's all it is. I was
              like that before I married your father . . . with
              very good reason as it turned out!

PAUL   No, it's more than that. I don't think we're
              right together.

OLIVE   Of course you are . . . she's a lovely girl.
              She's like one of the family already. Sensible,
              homely . . . just what you need. You can't go
              upsetting things now, it wouldn't be right.
              You know everybody's made arrangements.
              Your Aunt Mary's coming all the way from
              Leeds! It's just nerves, Paul, you take my
              word for it. You can't chop and change all
              your life, it's time you were settled.

PAUL   But I don't think I want to be. Even the word
              . . . settled. It's just another way of saying lie
              down and stop struggling. (*Looking out to sea
              again.*) He's still waving.

OLIVE   He can wave as much as he likes. He's not
              getting round me that easily!

PAUL   Would everybody be very upset if I called it
              off?

OLIVE   Of course they would! You can't go messing
              people about like that.

              (*There is a moment's silence as* OLIVE *returns
              to her crossword.*)

              (*Suddenly, with a complete change of tone.*)
              I'd be more upset if you weren't happy
              though. That's all I want, Paul . . . you to be
              happy.

PAUL	So, if I'm not sure about marrying Maureen?
OLIVE	Then you shouldn't marry her. Only you can decide, love.
PAUL	Thanks mum.

(PAUL *leans over and kisses* OLIVE *on the cheek. She returns to the crossword as* PAUL *looks out to sea again.*)

Why is he in the sea?

OLIVE	Don't be silly. You know he hates the water.
PAUL	He's paddling.
OLIVE	It can't be your father then. (*Looking up.*) It is him! He's waving again . . . what's he doing?
PAUL	I don't know.
OLIVE	(*panicking*) It's the rocks . . . he's been cut off. Quick, Paul . . . do something!
PAUL	He's all right. That's the high water mark.
OLIVE	But he doesn't know that. He's panicking.
PAUL	He'll soon find out. (*Seeing that* OLIVE *is genuinely worried.*) Oh, okay, I'll go and rescue him. I don't know what he's doing out there in the first place.
OLIVE	(*having second thoughts*) Are you sure that's high water?
PAUL	You can see it is!
OLIVE	Just leave him then. He can stand there for a bit. (*Smiling and waving out to sea.*) Cooee . . . cooee . . .

(*Music of the late 1960s plays as the lights fade.*)

ACT TWO

Scene One

The summer of 1969, one week later. Music of the late 1960s plays. ANNE *is sitting on the stile with* PAUL *by her side. He has his arm around her.* PAUL *is wearing jeans, an embroidered shirt and a headband. He is smoking a joint and gives the impression of being on a slightly different plane to the rest of the world. Music fades.*

ANNE   Do you really have to go back?

PAUL   Yeah, it's a drag. I told the old man I was only going away for a couple of days and it's been a week.

ANNE   What a week though. (*Kissing him.*) I wish it could last forever.

PAUL   Yeah.

        (PAUL *takes a huge drag on his joint and blows smoke towards* ANNE.)

ANNE   That smells disgusting!

PAUL   (*offering the joint to* ANNE) Hey, it's cool.

ANNE   No thanks, I'm particular about what I smoke!

PAUL   You've gotta live, man . . . this is the best.

ANNE   (*suspicious*) Who'd you get it from?

PAUL   Just a guy. (*Savouring the smoke.*) Pure Moroccan.

        (PAUL *takes a small foil wrapper from his pocket and offers it to* ANNE.)

        Get on it, babe.

        (ANNE *takes the wrapper from him and opens it as she walks away.* PAUL *takes another exaggerated drag.*)

Man, this stuff could make you fly!

(PAUL *starts giggling uncontrollably and climbs unsteadily on top of the stile.*)

ANNE   Careful, Paul!

(ANNE *sniffs the contents of the foil and smiles to herself. She dabs her finger into it and then puts her finger to her tongue.*)

PAUL   (*shouting*) Hey, world, I can fly!

(PAUL *leaps off the stile with arms outstretched and lands in a crumpled heap on the ground.*)

ANNE   (*running to him, anxious*) Paul!

PAUL   (*stunned, slowly lifting his head*) It's okay, man. Wow, some landing!

(PAUL *sits up slowly as* ANNE *kneels at his side.*)

ANNE   (*trying to keep a straight face*) Maybe you should try something stronger . . . stronger than Oxo anyway.

PAUL   (*dreamily*) Yeah. (*With slowly dawning realization.*) What?

ANNE   He sold you an Oxo cube . . . it's the oldest trick there is.

PAUL   (*in horror*) Oxo!

(PAUL *gradually changes back to his normal self, slowly recovering from his self-imposed high. He stubs the joint out fiercely.*)

Christ, I can't stand Oxo!

(PAUL *stands, trying to hide his embarrassment.*)

ANNE   How much did you pay for that?

PAUL   Me . . . what, pay for that? (*As casually as
            possible*.) Nothing . . . I was just fooling
            about, getting you going.

ANNE   You ought to be more careful, Paul, smoking
            all this stuff. You've been out of your skull
            all week!

PAUL   (*defensive*) You smoke it.

ANNE   Not the way you've been doing . . . and I
            certainly keep off the really hard stuff like
            Oxo!

PAUL   (*changing the subject rapidly*) I'd better get
            going. I can still see you again before you
            leave?

ANNE   Before I leave? Then what?

PAUL   I don't know . . . I'll have to think.

ANNE   Why do you need to think? Just pack your
            things and come with me . . . it's easy.

PAUL   Easy for you!

ANNE   And why should you be any different? Why
            should we tie ourselves down to the same old
            rut as our parents? Do you think that it's
            made them happy?

PAUL   I don't know. In their own way I suppose . . .
            I've never thought about it.

ANNE   That's because people don't think. Our
            parents, grandparents . . . they've never
            questioned anything, have they? They just
            drift through life obeying all the rules. Whose
            rules? It's time we changed the rules, and it's
            only our generation that can do it.

PAUL	Why ours? Why didn't they change things?
ANNE	Because they couldn't . . . they've been indoctrinated. We're better educated, we know what we want and how to go about getting it. We don't have to be tied down like them. It's the age of free love. (*Giggling.*) I rather like it.
PAUL	Yeah . . . I'd noticed.

(*They kiss passionately.*)

ANNE	Come with me.
PAUL	Christ, I wish I could! It's all so complicated. I mean, would it really work?
ANNE	Of course . . . why shouldn't it?
PAUL	Oh, just little things like money . . . food. I don't think I could live on lentil soup forever!
ANNE	It's not quite that bad! We make things . . . we grow things.
PAUL	So what use would I be? I don't know how to do anything.
ANNE	Why all the negative vibes? It'll work because we'll make it work. Trust me. We'd be together.
PAUL	I know.
ANNE	Don't think about it, just do it. It's your parents isn't it . . . you're worried about what your parents think?
PAUL	I just think I owe them something, that's all. Maybe I just don't want to let them down. Yes, they'd disapprove but they couldn't stop me.
ANNE	You can't spend your life trying to live up to their expectations, Paul. We can't just be

clones of our parents, we've got to be
ourselves. Okay, maybe they've got dreams
for us but we're entitled to our own dreams.
What about Maureen?

PAUL   Maureen! This last week I haven't even
thought about Maureen.

ANNE   (*half joking, half serious*) You've been too
busy with all the others.

PAUL   What others?

ANNE   Every girl at the festival! I've watched you
watching them . . . you've been like a little
kid in a sweet shop!

PAUL   There's only you . . . it's you that I want.

ANNE   Well then, there's nothing to stop you. Come
with me . . . please.

PAUL   I want to . . . I really do want to.

                (PAUL *kisses* ANNE *and then looks up
                suddenly.*)

                Oh, hell. It's my father!

ANNE   Where?

PAUL   Coming down the path. Come on, we'd better
move.

ANNE   What for?

PAUL   He can't see me here . . . with you! I was
supposed to be in Portsmouth . . . (*Worried.*)
or was it Plymouth?

ANNE   Didn't they know about the festival?

PAUL   It sometimes pays to keep them guessing.
Come on.

(PAUL *tries to drag* ANNE *over the stile but she resists.*)

ANNE   No. I'm not moving anywhere. If you're serious about wanting to be with me, then it's time a few people knew about it!

PAUL   I don't mind normal people knowing, but that's my father!

ANNE   He's got to know some time. At least now I'm here to back you up.

PAUL   I think I need the army to back me up!

(PAUL *half-heartedly tries to hide behind the stile as* ALBERT *enters stage left.* ANNE *moves to meet* ALBERT *who fails to recognize her and passes by her.*)

ANNE   Hallo, Mr Burton.

(ALBERT *stops and turns.* PAUL *continues to cower behind the stile, temporarily unnoticed.*)

ALBERT   Good afternoon. Do I know you?

ANNE   Anne. We met last week.

ALBERT   Ah. I thought your lot had gone now.

ANNE   I stayed on for a while.

ALBERT   Well, I won't keep you. I don't have a flask of tea on me if that's what you're after.

(ALBERT *turns to walk away.*)

ANNE   I stayed on with Paul.

ALBERT   (*turning*) With who!

ANNE   Your son, Paul. I believe you've met. Paul, say hello to your father.

ALBERT   Paul!

PAUL   (*climbing back over the stile with an
             uncertain sheepish expression*) Hi, dad.

ALBERT   You're in Portsmouth!

PAUL   No I'm not . . . I'm here.

ALBERT   I can see that, I can see you're here. But
             you're in Portsmouth . . . that's where you
             said you were!

PAUL   I changed my mind, that's all.

ANNE   No you didn't.

PAUL   Yes I did.

ANNE   You didn't!

ALBERT   He did . . . he didn't! Is this a bloody
             pantomime or what! (*To* PAUL.) Is there
             something wrong with your head?

PAUL   I'm just confused.

ALBERT   I know that . . . that's obvious. But I don't
             mean the inside of your head, I mean the
             outside.

PAUL   Oh, this. (*Fingering the headband.*) It's a
             symbol, it shows . . . it shows . . . (*To* ANNE.)
             What does it show again?

ANNE   It shows that you're free . . . independent.
             That you don't have to conform. It shows that
             you're not one of *them* anymore.

ALBERT   Pardon me, young lady, but I'd say it shows
             that he *is* one of them. Get the bloody thing
             off. You look like a kamikaze pilot.

PAUL   (*to* ANNE) I'm not sure this is such a good
             idea.

ANNE	You can't give in at the first bit of pressure! We've all had to go through it at some time. Think for yourself.
ALBERT	He's never had to think for himself. Come on, let's have you home.
ANNE	In that case think of me.
ALBERT	And why should he be thinking of you! Your Maureen's been on to us. Every half hour for the last few days. Is he back yet . . . has he rung? And your mother's been there, trying to make excuses for you.
PAUL	(*sadly*) She didn't need to make excuses. I'll see her myself.
ALBERT	And what tale are you going to spin her? Same rubbish you told us! I've been worked off my feet this last week while you've been gadding off God knows where!
PAUL	I'll tell her the truth.
ALBERT	Oh, the truth. We're getting to the truth now are we? So what is it then . . . what is the truth?
PAUL	I'll tell her it's finished.
ALBERT	It's what!
PAUL	I can't go through with it. I've found other things . . . different things that I want to do. (*Putting his arm around* ANNE.) Other people I want to be with.
ALBERT	Other things, other people! And what about your mother and me, where does that leave us then?
PAUL	Look. I know it's difficult for you to understand . . .

ALBERT   You're bloody right it is!

PAUL   . . . but I'm not trying to hurt anybody. That's
                the last thing I want. It's just time that I did
                something for myself, that's all . . .
                something that I want to do.

ALBERT   (*to* ANNE) I suppose you're behind this?

PAUL   It's not Anne's fault.

ALBERT   I'm talking to her. Well, come on . . . it's all
                your idea is it?

ANNE   It's Paul's choice. I just showed him some
                different options.

ALBERT   Different options! Let me tell you something,
                young lady. He doesn't need your different
                options. I give him all the options he needs. I
                have done since he was this high. I've fed
                him, I've clothed him . . . and when he was
                old enough I gave him a job. A bloody good
                job. A job most lads his age could only dream
                of. A job in my business. And I'll tell you
                something else. In a few years time it'll be
                his business. Oh, we're not that big, I'll grant
                you that . . . but it matters to me . . . and to
                him. So, Paul, I suggest you say your
                goodbyes and we'll be on our way.

                (PAUL *looks at* ALBERT *for several seconds and
                then at* ANNE.)

                We haven't got all day.

PAUL   I'm sorry, Dad, I can't. Last week, last month
                . . . maybe. Now I can't. I've got to go and do
                my own thing. I need my own space.

ALBERT   By the sound of it you've got quite enough
                space between your ears! You're wanting to
                go off with her!

PAUL	With Anne . . . she's not a her. Well she is, but . . .
ALBERT	But you're not even sure about that!

(*During the following passage* ALBERT *occasionally touches his chest with an uneasy expression.*)

ANNE	I'm not forcing you into anything, Paul. I'd understand.
PAUL	Give me a few minutes . . . on my own with my dad.
ANNE	Just remember, it's your choice. Don't let anybody make you do something that you don't want.
PAUL	I know what I want. I won't be long.
ANNE	I'll wait on the beach. (*Kissing* PAUL.) Be yourself. I'll maybe see you later, Mr Burton.
ALBERT	I should very much doubt that.

(ANNE *exits.*)

Right, Paul. Let's get off, and we'll have no more of this rubbish.

PAUL	I'm serious, dad. I'm leaving with Anne.
ALBERT	Just have some bloody sense will you! What has she got to offer you? Your life's here, with us . . . it always has been. Where would you go?
PAUL	A commune. She lives in a commune.
ALBERT	A commune! What the hell's one of those?
PAUL	Everybody shares everything. It's how we should all be.

ALBERT   Sharing everything? They're living in a
                bloody dream world! I've worked bloody hard
                for what I've got. I wouldn't go sharing it
                with any Tom, Dick or Harry. I built it up
                from nothing because it's what I wanted . . .
                so I'd have something to pass on to you when
                the time came.

PAUL   That was your choice though, dad, not mine.
                All I'm saying is that I want the chance to do
                things in my own way . . . make my own life.

ALBERT   And what makes you think this commune
                business is right? If you hadn't met Loopy
                Lilly you'd never have thought of it.

PAUL   Insulting her doesn't help! Maybe you've got
                a right to have a go at me, but not Anne. You
                don't even know her. It's the only way you
                know, isn't it? If you don't understand
                something pull it to pieces, call it names! It's
                pathetic.

ALBERT   So that's it is it, pathetic! That's all I mean to
                you?

PAUL   Dad, I don't want to argue with you. I just
                want you to see my point of view. Look,
                maybe I am making a mistake, but I've got to
                try. If it doesn't work out I'll come back, I
                promise.

ALBERT   And that's your point of view is it? Your high
                and mighty point of view? Right, well I'll
                make *you* a promise. If you go off with her, I
                don't want you back. You can say goodbye to
                it all because as far as I'm concerned you're
                no son of mine. You'll never be part of my
                family again . . . you won't get a penny out of
                the business. (*He puts his hand to his chest
                and grimaces.*) What do you think to that!

PAUL   Is that really the only thing you can think of
                . . . resort to blackmail!

ALBERT	I'm just stating fact, there's no blackmail.
PAUL	Oh no, just emotional, financial! Well, if that's the way it's got to be, okay. You can do what you like with the business . . . it was always yours, not mine. But you haven't got the right to decide about the family. What about mum, doesn't she have a say?
ALBERT	And what say does she have in all this rubbish you're talking!
PAUL	I'll talk to her . . . I'll explain. At least she might be prepared to listen!
ALBERT	It'll break her heart . . . you know that?
PAUL	Isn't that what you're trying to do to me? Making me choose between you and Anne? If I had kids I could never do that to them. You don't deserve to be a father!
ALBERT	I'll tell you something, Paul. For the first time in my life I wish I wasn't.
PAUL	Look, I'm not doing this to hurt anybody. You should be proud of the fact that I'm able to think for myself.
ALBERT	Proud! You expect me to be proud of you!
	(ALBERT *clutches his chest again and tries to reach into his jacket pocket for some tablets. He staggers slightly and* PAUL *tries to put his hand out to steady him.*)
PAUL	Dad, what's wrong? Dad!
ALBERT	(*pushing* PAUL *away and taking a tablet*) Get your bloody hands off me! I don't need you. Get back to her, where you belong!

(ALBERT *walks unsteadily to the stile. As he tries to lift a leg onto it he slumps over it.*)

Paul! Help me, Paul!

(*The lights black out. When the lights rise, it's the following day.* PAUL *and* ANNE *are together.* PAUL *has a small camera in his hand. A large packed bag belonging to* ANNE *is on the ground. There is a mixed sense of closeness and despair in both of them.*)

ANNE   So he is going to be all right?

PAUL   The hospital said it's too early to say, but yes, they think so.

ANNE   I feel kind of responsible somehow.

PAUL   How do you think I feel! The doctor said it could have happened at any time. Apparently he's had a problem for ages . . . he's been taking tablets. He didn't even tell my mum!

ANNE   Will you tell her I'm sorry? I suppose she blames me as well.

PAUL   I haven't told her anything yet . . . not about the argument. I will do, but not yet.

(*There is a pause for a few seconds.*)

ANNE   This is it then.

PAUL   I'm sorry but I can't come with you . . . not at the moment. Couldn't you stay for a while longer?

ANNE   I can't, not like this. It's . . . it's all wrong.

PAUL   I will come after you . . . eventually. If I can get things sorted out here . . . if my dad's all right.

ANNE   (*sadly*) It'd be great to see you . . . but I won't, I know that.

PAUL   Course you will!

ANNE   (*slowly*) Your father was right. You belong
            here. I'm not certain you'll find everything
            you need, but you'll stay.

PAUL   (*desperately*) Don't say that! Change your
            mind. Stay here with me . . . we could sort
            everything out.

ANNE   I can't.

PAUL   Why not? I don't want you to go . . . you
            can't go! We could live together . . . here.

ANNE   But that wouldn't be right for me. I want to
            see you again, Paul, more than you realize,
            but not here . . . not like this. When you're
            ready . . . if you're ready, you know where to
            find me.

            (PAUL *clings despairingly to* ANNE *and they
            kiss.*)

            I'm sorry.

PAUL   Yeah.

ANNE   (*tearfully*) I've got to go.

            (ANNE *breaks away from* PAUL *and moves
            away from him, picking up her bag.*)

PAUL   I *will* see you again.

            (ANNE *tries to smile but gently shakes her
            head, then hurriedly turns to leave.* PAUL
            raises the camera to his eye.)

PAUL   (*calling*) Anne!

            (As ANNE *turns her face to* PAUL *he takes a
            photograph while the lights fade and music of
            the late 1960s plays, then fades into music of
            the 1990s.*)

Scene Two

The year is 1996, a week after the events of Act One, Scene One. The bench is back in position. ANNE *and* PAUL *are having a picnic. A picnic hamper is open and food and drink are scattered around it. Both* ANNE *and* PAUL *are casually dressed with* ANNE *again looking immaculate. The most dramatic difference is in* PAUL *who has bought new clothes. Music fades.*

ANNE   It all seems so long ago . . . 1969.

PAUL   I don't know. Sometimes it feels like a lifetime. . . sometimes it feels like yesterday.

ANNE   What exactly happened after I left?

PAUL   It was all somewhat hectic. Dad was in hospital for a couple of weeks. When he came out it was obvious he'd never do much in the business any more. It was more mental than physical though. His body was fine but he decided to play safe and devoted all his energy to his mouth!

ANNE   I think I can picture that.

PAUL   He adopted the air of a martyr. He bought an old second-hand wheelchair and insisted on being pushed everywhere . . . only when it suited him, mind. A wheel fell off once and he carried the chair two miles to complain!

ANNE   I suppose you never gave me a second thought, after I'd gone.

PAUL   That's not true. It just wasn't possible . . . I had to marry Maureen.

ANNE   Were they all putting pressure on you?

PAUL   Not directly, no. But with dad on the sidelines I just got pulled into the business more. For a few weeks I thought of all the possible alternatives . . . selling up, all kinds of things. Then Maureen hit me with the bombshell.

(ANNE *looks at* PAUL *quizzically.*)

Al! After that it was all something of a forgone conclusion. The wedding was an absolute disaster! At least, the reception was.

ANNE   In what way?

PAUL   Maureen's mum and my mum decided to do the catering themselves. We might have got away with that but I had an aunt who came down from Leeds especially for the wedding. Now, she was something of an expert on pork pies.

ANNE   On what?

PAUL   Pork pies. Every family get-together I can remember she'd be there, passing comment on the quality. It seems that the pork pies on this occasion weren't up to scratch and she just wouldn't shut up about it. My side of the family could take it all in their stride, but Maureen's turned very nasty. Feelings ran so high that we had to abandon the reception at half-time due to crowd trouble.

ANNE   (*laughing*) Why should anybody take such an interest in pork pies?

PAUL   Most families have got an authority on something . . . it's what makes family get-togethers tolerable, you can play "spot the expert". She'd go down very well on "Mastermind" . . . specialist subject, the life and times of a pork pie. Family gossip has it that it all started after a mad fling with a pork butcher from Barnsley. Anyway, the final outcome was that Maureen wouldn't speak to me for the first week of the honeymoon.

ANNE   Maybe I made a wise choice, remaining in
                unwedded bliss.

PAUL   It did get better! (*Holding a bottle of wine
                over* ANNE'S *glass*.) Top up?

ANNE   No thanks.

PAUL   But you've only had one!

ANNE   I'm driving, aren't I? London, remember?

PAUL   (*turning up his nose and examining the
                contents of the bottle*) Have I drunk all this?

ANNE   You made it look effortless.

PAUL   I've been practising for years. This week
                seems to have flown. Do you have to go?

ANNE   I promise I'll be back on Thursday.

PAUL   (*pouring wine for himself*) Just keep off the
                M25, otherwise you won't be *there* by
                Thursday!

                (*There is silence for a few seconds, each of
                them lost in their own thoughts.*)

                What are you thinking?

ANNE   Nothing much. Just admiring the view. You?

PAUL   (*looking pointedly at* ANNE) Much the same.

ANNE   (*quickly*) I don't think it's really changed.

PAUL   It has up here, caravans and everything. Not
                down there though. That's why I like it here
                . . . the sea never changes. It just carries on as
                though none of us matter. I suppose we're
                even trying to ruin that . . . pollution and
                everything. Mankind seems to have a fatal
                desire to destroy everything it sees.

ANNE   You didn't like living here before.

PAUL

No, it wasn't that. There were just so many other things that I wanted to do . . . I didn't think I could ever do them here.

ANNE

And did you?

PAUL

Some of them. Not all. That sounds ungrateful. I'm not ungrateful . . . I just sometimes wonder.

ANNE

(*uncertain*) Why did you keep the photograph?

PAUL

(*evasive*) I always keep photographs. If they ever decide to do a "This Is Your Life" on me, they could be very useful.

ANNE

Be serious for a minute. You had it on you . . . when you met Julie.

PAUL

(*after a pause*) I knew you'd ask me that eventually. I don't know how to answer it. Not without embarrassing you . . . or me for that matter.

ANNE

Just be honest. Honesty shouldn't embarrass us.

PAUL

I'm not entirely sure that honesty's always the best policy.

ANNE

What use are lies?

PAUL

I'm not advocating dishonesty. I just think complete honesty is sometimes rather dangerous. It should only be practiced between consenting adults.

ANNE

I'm over eighteen . . . just.

PAUL

I don't think you'll like it somehow.

ANNE

I'll like it even less if you don't tell me.

(PAUL *collects his thoughts for a few seconds.*)

PAUL

I suppose . . . I suppose I never stopped thinking about you. (*Pause.*) Never stopped loving you.

ANNE   What!

PAUL   I told you that you wouldn't like it.

ANNE   (*surprised rather than annoyed*) But you were
            married . . . how could you keep thinking of
            me all this time?

PAUL   I suppose you think it makes me seem
            unfaithful to Maureen.

ANNE   Maybe.

PAUL   I did love Maureen. I wasn't sure of that when
            we got married . . . but I did love her. I'd give
            anything in the world to have her back, but
            nothing's going to bring her back, is it?

ANNE   Did she ever know anything about me?

PAUL   Nobody did except dad. I didn't tell anybody
            about the argument that put him in hospital,
            not even mum. It was just an unsaid pact
            between him and me . . . it was never
            mentioned again. It was as though nothing
            had ever happened . . . except for the
            photograph. I know I should have thrown it
            away. Every time I looked at it I felt guilty,
            as though I was being unfaithful . . . but I
            wasn't. It is possible to be in love with two
            people at the same time.

ANNE   Is it?

PAUL   People are different . . . so is love.

ANNE   But I wasn't around. I was just a face on a
            photograph. You knew you wouldn't see me
            again.

PAUL   Maybe that's why it seemed acceptable. I
            could go on loving you without ever having to
            choose.

ANNE	But you did choose. When you married Maureen you made your choice.
PAUL	Was it a choice?
ANNE	Yes, it was.
PAUL	Anyway, you didn't expect to see me again.
ANNE	I didn't expect, no . . . but I desperately wanted to. I didn't even have a photograph. When I moved on from the commune . . . that was because of you.
PAUL	Why?
ANNE	You talk about how you felt . . . it's all you! You never had a thought for the effect you might have had on me? I sat in the commune for months waiting for you to come along. I knew you wouldn't, but I so desperately wanted you to. In the end the only way out was to move away.
PAUL	But then I couldn't have contacted you.
ANNE	Exactly. I was free of you . . . no more wondering, no more hoping. Yes, I still had your address but I knew that I could never contact you. If it was going to work it had to be the other way round.
PAUL	I thought about you a lot . . .
ANNE	When I was feeling lonely and hurt I couldn't hug your thoughts!
PAUL	I'm sorry. I never meant to hurt you.
ANNE	I think it's a little too late for tears, don't you? As I said, it's all a long time ago.
PAUL	Long time ago . . . yesterday. What about now?
ANNE	Now? We're different people, both of us.

PAUL   Do you think so? I'm not sure that people
            ever change that much. Maybe their
            circumstances change but they're the same
            underneath all the wrapping.

ANNE   Well, I've changed. My way of going about
            things certainly has.

PAUL   Perhaps you've just advanced . . . moved on.
            Football players graduate to managers, actors
            become directors, prats become politicians.
            They're all still doing the same thing but
            from a different angle.

            (JULIE *and* AL *enter, stage left.*)

            Talking of prats, here's Al!

AL   Yo. We've come to brighten up your day.

PAUL   It was fairly cloudless until you appeared over
            the horizon.

AL   Ooh, nasty. The rapier wit! (*To* JULIE.) See
            what I've got to live with!

ANNE   Where's Sam?

JULIE   She's gone back to the caravan to get
            changed. She went for a swim.

ANNE   Just her?

JULIE   We're not that stupid . . . it's freezing!

AL   Sam thought it might cure her hangover. She
            can't take the pace. I whisked them round all
            the local high spots last night.

JULIE   It took all of twenty minutes. Then we
            thrashed him at pool.

AL   Only because I was using the bent cue.
            Anyway, the table's not level, one of the legs
            is propped on beer mats!

PAUL	My whole life's like that . . . distinctly wobbly and held up with little packing pieces. I thought you were telling me the other day that you were very good at "playing the angles".
AL	When it comes to business, yes. You concentrate on the smart cracks, I'll concentrate on making us millionaires. Any wine left?
PAUL	(*turning the bottle upside down*) Sorry.
AL	Oh, thank you very much. I'm gasping.
PAUL	I'm not a mobile wine bar! (*Relenting.*) There's another bottle in there. (*Indicating the picnic basket.*)
AL	Awesome! You're a winner, dad.
PAUL	Only when you want something and I've got it.
ANNE	Al's like that as well? I thought it was just Julie.
PAUL	It's not just these two, it's the whole generation of them! The kodak kids.
ANNE	Kodak kids?
PAUL	Kodak instamatic. They want everything instantly and to work automatically.
AL	(*pulling a wine bottle from the picnic basket*) Sharp as a knife isn't he? (*Inspecting the bottle dubiously and reading the label.*) What's this supposed to be? "Fine Country Wine".
PAUL	It's good stuff . . . British.
AL	So's tap water and I never dare drink that either. (*To* JULIE.) Want to risk it?
JULIE	I will if you will.

(AL *opens the bottle and pours a glass for*
JULIE *and one for himself.*)

PAUL   (*to* ANNE) See? I provide him with everything
            his heart could desire and that's the thanks I
            get.

AL   It's my stomach lining I'm worried about, not
            my heart. (*Examining the bottle again and
            talking to* JULIE.) This is his idea of wild
            extravagant living!

PAUL   They expect everything on a plate.

AL   Like what?

PAUL   Everything! What did you want as soon as you
            reached seventeen?

AL   Car of course.

PAUL   And who was expected to provide it?

AL   You. I didn't have the money.

PAUL   I rest my case.

AL   It's not a very fair example though is it! If
            you were talking about luxuries fair enough,
            b it a car's an essential, isn't it? Christ, we're
            not living in the dark ages.

PAUL   But that's what I'm saying. What were
            luxuries for us, you regard as some sort of
            birthright.

JULIE   Mum wouldn't buy me a car.

AL   What! (*Joking.*) Is that any way to treat a
            child? I hope you left home immediately.

ANNE   That was the plan. It didn't work.

JULIE   (*indignant*) You were sorry to see me go when
            I went to college.

ANNE   Only because I wanted you to work and
        support me in the manner in which I have to
        support myself.

PAUL   I sent Al to college but they sent him back!

AL   All this criticism is just jealousy you know.
        He can't stand the fact that I understand
        modern technology and he can't.

PAUL   I wouldn't want to.

AL   You should see him with the computers . . .
        he even looks at the coffee vending machine
        as though it was "The Thing From Outer
        Space"!

PAUL   If you've got an organized mind and the will
        to get stuck in, you don't need computers . . .
        or coffee machines.

AL   They save time, they save money and they
        save effort.

PAUL   Exactly . . . effort. Nobody wants to do
        anything themselves any more. A machine's
        got to do it. Mister fix-it has been replaced by
        mister fax-it.

AL   Sam's doing computer studies. I said I'd take
        her round later and show her the system we've
        got in.

PAUL   That's another thing. Technology has taken
        all the romance out of life. In your
        grandfather's day you could invite a young
        lady up to see your etchings. In my day it
        was, "Come and listen to my records". Now
        it's, "Want to see my floppy disk?"

AL   Hard disks are better.

PAUL   We won't go into that if you don't mind.

AL   Come on Jules, are you ready?

JULIE   Okay. Aren't you finishing your drink?

AL   No. Dad can re-lacquer the bench with it.

PAUL   Where are you going now?

AL   Won't be long. I said I'd drive Sam over to
              the cash point in town. Then we're going to
              chill out back at the caravan.

ANNE   I'll be gone by the time you get back. I'll see
              you in a few days.

JULIE   (*giving* ANNE *a farewell kiss*) Okay. Take
              care.

ANNE   I will. Just you and Sam be sensible.

JULIE   Mum. I can look after myself!

ANNE   I know, but just be careful, that's all.

AL   I'll keep an eye on them. See you later.

              (JULIE *and* AL *exit left in a chorus of
              goodbyes.*)

ANNE   Would you keep an eye on them as well?

PAUL   Course I will. Anyway, as long as Al's seeing
              Sam they'll be okay. He's not as daft as he
              looks.

ANNE   Sorry, I wasn't suggesting . . . did you really
              mean all that about their generation?

PAUL   What did I say? . . . I tend to ramble when Al
              gets me going.

ANNE   Their attitudes. Expecting everything as a
              right.

PAUL   I'm not sure. I joke about it but I've got a
              sneaking suspicion that I actually mean it.

They're certainly different to us, I know that. (*Crossing to pick up* AL'S *abandoned wine*.) They pick and choose.

ANNE   Only because they've got more to choose from.

PAUL   I put it down to not making Al eat his greens when he was little! (*Taking a sip of wine and grimacing*.) Lovely stuff, this.

ANNE   Every generation takes great pleasure in trying to shock the previous generation. That doesn't make them any better or worse.

PAUL   I just wonder about their values, that's all. We seem to have gone backwards. When we were young, in the 60s, material things weren't supposed to matter.

ANNE   That's what we said, but I don't think it's what we meant. All we were really interested in was having a good time . . . without any of the responsibilities of living in the real world.

PAUL   Were we really that cynical?

ANNE   I think so.

PAUL   So why didn't it work then? Why didn't *I* have a good time!

ANNE   You didn't know how to.

PAUL   That was meant to be a humorous aside.

ANNE   Oh, sorry. It did have a ring of truth though didn't it! Anyway, I'm not saying it was all a waste of time. At least we managed to bring things out into the open more. That's why Julie and Al are like they are now. They don't try to hide things or justify things . . . we've got past all that now. They say exactly what they think.

PAUL   I often wish Al wouldn't. It's a bit
            disappointing though . . . I thought we'd
            achieved a bit more than that.

ANNE   Thought *we'd* achieved more? I'm not sure
            that *we* achieved anything really. We were
            just hangers-on . . . part-time hippies . . . .

PAUL   You weren't. You were prepared to stand up
            for what you believed in.

ANNE   We didn't stand up for anything. It was the
            age of the great sit-in, remember.

PAUL   You know what I mean. That was one thing I
            really admired about you. Okay, I admit that I
            was only a minor flower person . . . no more
            than a potted plant, but you did the whole lot.

ANNE   And then in the end we all gave up and went
            off and became bank managers and
            accountants just like out parents . . .
            (*Bitterly.*) . . . or ruined the rest of our lives.

PAUL   You're right about one thing. You have
            changed.

ANNE   Maybe I had good reason to. I just think that
            we had a rather over-inflated opinion of
            ourselves. (*Quietly.*) All this time you've
            been carrying that photograph around. You
            haven't been in love with me, you've been in
            love with what you thought I was.

PAUL   No. At first maybe . . . but there's something
            you've left out of your calculation. I'm not in
            love with the girl in the photograph any more.

ANNE   (*not sure whether to be hurt or pleased*)   See
            . . . it was all a stupid mistake.

PAUL   Now . . . now I'm in love with the lady she
            turned in to.

(PAUL *takes* ANNE'S *hand and they look at each other for a few seconds.*)

ANNE   I'm not sure what I can say to that.

PAUL   Don't say anything.

(PAUL *kisses her lightly on the lips.*)

ANNE   I still don't know what to say.

PAUL   Does it shock you that much?

ANNE   No, it doesn't shock me. Just surprises me that's all. (*Looking at her watch.*) Paul, I've got to get going.

PAUL   Not until you've told me what you think.

ANNE   I can't tell you what I think . . . not at the moment.

PAUL   So what's happened to all this honesty you thought was such a good idea?

ANNE   I can't tell you because I don't know. Look . . . it's all too sudden.

PAUL   But you'll think about what I said, while you're away?

ANNE   Of course I'll think about it . . . how could I do anything but think about it! I can't promise anything.

PAUL   I know that, but remember . . . I meant it. Come on, we'll pack these things and I'll walk you to your car.

(ANNE *and* PAUL *start packing things into the picnic basket.*)

Why did you decide to come back here for a holiday?

ANNE   It just seemed like a good place to come. Julie
                hadn't been here before. (*Looking at* PAUL.) It
                wasn't for any other reason.

PAUL   (*blankly*) No.

ANNE   (*gently*) Look, my mind isn't as tortured or
                twisted or devious as yours. I don't plan my
                life around things that happened twenty-odd
                years ago.

PAUL   Is that what you think? Tortured, twisted?

ANNE   I'm sorry, that was a cruel thing to say. I
                didn't mean it to sound like that.

                (*The basket is now packed except for the
                empty wine bottle which* PAUL *fiddles with
                nervously.*)

PAUL   I probably asked for it. I seem to have an
                unerring ability to make a complete fool of
                myself. You'd think I'd have grown out of it
                by now.

ANNE   Don't put yourself down! Life's too full of
                other people who are quite prepared to do that
                for you. (*Carefully.*) I'll be quite honest.
                When we first met, I was very attracted to you
                . . . then it all just ended, suddenly. These last
                few days I've felt the same attraction . . . no,
                not the same, but . . . something. But it's too
                early. You want to pick up exactly where we
                left off. I can't do that. I've got to start again.

PAUL   But there is a chance?

ANNE   A chance of what? What are you actually
                looking for? We're still virtually strangers.

PAUL   (*embarrassed*) I have made a fool of myself.

ANNE   No you haven't. (*Looking at her watch.*) It's
                getting late. Put that bottle in and we'll go.

PAUL   That's what I mean . . . I have made a fool of myself. I've got my finger stuck!

                (ANNE *looks down at the bottle which* PAUL *displays sheepishly, attached to his finger.*)

ANNE   (*laughing*) You idiot! Is it really stuck?

PAUL   Completely and utterly.

ANNE   How did you manage that?

PAUL   I've been practising for years.

                (ANNE *tugs at the bottle.*)

ANNE   It won't move.

PAUL   I know that!

ANNE   Let's go to the caravan. We'd better try it under the tap or something. You're impossible!

                (*On impulse,* ANNE *kisses* PAUL *quickly and then, picking up the basket, leads him off.*)

                You're worse than a five year old!

                (*The lights fade as music of the 1990s plays. When the lights rise, it's about half an hour later. Music fades.* PAUL *sits on the bench with the picnic basket by his side. He has a large plaster on his finger and is muttering quietly to the plaque. He doesn't notice* JULIE *enter. She stands for a second watching him.*)

JULIE   I often talk to myself as well.

PAUL   (*jumping, surprised by her presence*) Julie, don't do that! I thought he was answering back!

JULIE   Who?

PAUL	I wasn't talking to myself, I was having a quiet chat with my father.
JULIE	Sorry. Would you rather I left?
PAUL	No, you're fine. He wasn't being very communicative anyway.
JULIE	He sometimes is?
PAUL	Positively chatty on occasions. Actually, when he's quiet it's a good sign. He makes the biggest fuss when he thinks I'm making a mistake . . . that's most of the time.
JULIE	Has mum gone?
PAUL	Yes, about ten minutes ago. I was just having a rest before I head back home. It's a sign of old age. When you're young you have a sit down when you get somewhere. When you get old you have a sit down before you set off!
JULIE	(*noticing the plaster*) What happened to your finger?
PAUL	Your mum hit the bottle.
JULIE	What! Was she okay to drive?
PAUL	I don't mean hit the bottle literally . . . yes I do. It was on my finger.
JULIE	(*in disbelief*) Bottle on your finger . . . whatever turns you on! Al's taken Sam off to look at his computers.
PAUL	That obviously didn't turn you on. Not interested in interfacing with his peripherals or whatever the phrase is?
JULIE	Definitely not. I just use them, I don't particularly want to know what they eat for breakfast.
PAUL	I bet they can manage three Shredded Wheat!

JULIE   Doesn't Al drive fast! I'm terrified of getting
                 in the car with him.

PAUL   I never go anywhere if he's driving. My
                 whole life flashes past . . . then he overtakes
                 it again! (*Sadly.*) One of these days he's going
                 to meet himself coming against where he's
                 wenting away from. There'll be a hell of a
                 bang.

JULIE   He's nice though, apart from his driving.
                 (*Probing.*) How are you and mum getting
                 along?

PAUL   I think you should ask her. I'm not authorized
                 to issue unilateral communiqués.

JULIE   She never tells me anything.

PAUL   She doesn't tell me a lot!

JULIE   She still thinks I'm a kid.

PAUL   Parents always do. They mean well.

JULIE   But there are limits . . . I *am* twenty-six.

                 (PAUL *is startled by this fact, and a train of
                 thought is suddenly triggered. He tries to act
                 casually.*)

PAUL   Twenty-six?

JULIE   Old isn't it!

PAUL   Are you sure you're twenty-six?

JULIE   Of course I am, I've been keeping count.
                 Why?

PAUL   Nothing. I just thought your mum told me you
                 were twenty-five, that's all. I probably
                 misheard.

JULIE   She hates me getting older . . . it makes her
             feel ancient. She can't accept that I'm old
             enough to be independent.

PAUL   When's your birthday exactly? (*Hurriedly.*)
             I'll send you a card.

JULIE   19th of May. I'm a Taurus.

PAUL   (*frantically working dates out in his head*)
             Load of bull . . . star signs.

JULIE   Do you think so? I suppose I agree with you. I
             only believe them when they say something
             nice.

PAUL   So, you were born in May 1970?

JULIE   Yeah. Somebody had to be.

PAUL   I was just thinking it makes you almost the
             same as Al. There's only a few weeks in it.

JULIE   Yes, I know. (*Moving to the cliff edge.*) It's
             beautiful here, isn't it . . . it's like . . . like
             you can really breathe. I walk along the cliff
             top and I feel as free as a bird. It's as though
             I belong here somehow. (*Turning back to*
             PAUL *and laughing.*) You belong here.

PAUL   Why?

JULIE   It's just you . . . you fit. Everybody has a
             place . . . your place is here.

PAUL   (*trying to be casual*) What about your father?
             Do you see much of him?

JULIE   You must be joking. I've never even met him.
             It's sad really but . . . maybe I wouldn't want
             to meet him. He'd probably be a terrible
             disappointment. Anyway, he obviously never
             cared about me, so why should I care about
             him!

PAUL   You know a bit about him though?

JULIE	Mum never mentions him. (*Excited, with a sudden thought.*) Hey, what about you?
PAUL	(*in horror*) What!
JULIE	Maybe you can tell me something. You and mum go back a long way . . . mid-60s, I think she said.
PAUL	Mid-60s. Yes, it must have been . . . we met in, er . . . (*Waiting for a prompt.*)
JULIE	Wales, wasn't it?
PAUL	Yes, Wales, that's right.
JULIE	So?
PAUL	I'm sorry, I can't really help. It must have all happened after my time. It certainly wasn't . . . I mean, I didn't . . .
JULIE	I think Mum's ashamed of it. All she's ever said was that it happened while she was away somewhere . . . a rock concert or something.

(PAUL *moves away, lost in thought.*)

They used to have something like that round here didn't they?

(PAUL *is slow to react. Then he realizes that* JULIE *was still talking to him.*)

PAUL	Sorry . . . what did you say?
JULIE	They used to have rock festivals around here.
PAUL	Yes, I believe so. (*Hurriedly.*) I don't know much about them . . . not really my kind of thing.
JULIE	What was your kind of thing? Everything I've heard about the sixties . . . I bet it was really wild.

(PAUL *is stunned by the revelations and clumsily tries to distance himself from anything connected with* ANNE.)

PAUL Wild! No, I don't think so. I wasn't wild. I just used to stay at home and listen to classical music. I certainly never went anywhere near those rock festivals . . . perish the thought, awful things!

JULIE You like classical music?

PAUL Oh, I'm a great fan.

JULIE That's great . . . so am I. What do you like?

PAUL Like? (*Struggling for inspiration.*) All sorts. I'll listen to anything.

JULIE But you must have favourites.

PAUL Not really. Er, Mozart I think . . . I probably like him best. He wrote that er . . . well, he wrote all sorts really, didn't he? Very clever. Very good.

JULIE We seem to have so much in common, don't we?

PAUL Do we? No, I wouldn't have thought so. Actually I'm more interested in jazz these days. (*Looking at his watch.*) God, is that the time?

JULIE The first time I saw you here, I knew instinctively that you were okay. I wouldn't normally talk to a complete stranger like that but it just seemed quite natural somehow. Almost as though we'd met before . . . like an old friend.

PAUL (*glancing at his watch again, increasingly anxious to get away from* JULIE) I must get going . . . very important things to do.

JULIE	Or a relative. An uncle that you haven't seen for years and years.
PAUL	(*panicking*) But we're not!
JULIE	Not what?
PAUL	Related. We're not connected at all . . . other than by common interests . . . which we haven't really got . . . me liking jazz. Not related.
JULIE	(*puzzled*) Of course we're not.
PAUL	No, course we're not. Look, I'll see you in the next day or so. I've got to dash, it's the cat . . . Tiddles.
JULIE	You should get a litter tray.
PAUL	(*lost in his own thoughts*) What?
JULIE	A litter tray, or a cat flap.
PAUL	Yes, I am rather.
JULIE	What?
PAUL	In a flap . . . about the cat.
JULIE	No, a cat flap. Are you feeling okay?
PAUL	Yes, fine . . . right. Anyway, must get off. It'll need feeding . . . the cat.
JULIE	See you sometime then.
PAUL	Fine . . . absolutely. Yes.

(PAUL *stands and looks at* JULIE *for just a fraction too long before recovering his thoughts.*)

In a day or two.

(PAUL *exits hurriedly over the stile leaving* JULIE *watching him with a rather bemused expression. She shrugs her shoulders and exits*

stage left. A few seconds later PAUL *enters
again looking anxiously to make sure that*
JULIE *has left. He leans on the bench and
glances at the plaque.)*

(*desperately*) She didn't tell me! Why the hell
didn't she tell me?

(PAUL *sits wearily on the bench, hiding his
head in his hands as the lights fade. When the
lights rise, it is some time later and* PAUL *is
still sitting on the bench, head in hands.* AL
enters left, looking surprised to see PAUL
there.)

AL	I've been looking for you.
PAUL	What?
AL	I've been looking for you. I rang home, you weren't there. How long have you been sat here?
PAUL	Oh, just a while, I don't know.
AL	Julie was worried about you. She said you were acting odd.
PAUL	Par for the course.
AL	Then when she said you'd gone home to feed the cat!
PAUL	So?
AL	We haven't got a cat! And what's all this about classical music and jazz?
PAUL	I just wanted to be on my own for a while.
AL	Has something happened?
PAUL	Like what? No, nothing's happened. I just wanted some peace and quiet. Did you impress Sam?

AL	I think so. She thought I'd got everything spot on.
PAUL	You have. You've done well.
AL	Pity Julie didn't come along though . . . I'd rather impress her.
PAUL	Why? It's Sam you've been trying to chat up isn't it?
AL	Only 'cos I met her first in the disco. I didn't know about Julie then. It's her I fancy, but having originally got off with Sam I'm having to play it a bit carefully.
PAUL	(*cautiously*) I thought you were just friends with Julie.
AL	I am . . . at the moment.
PAUL	(*firmly*) That's the way it's got to stay.
AL	Why, I'm a free agent!
PAUL	It wouldn't be right. It's unfair to Sam . . . you're just using her.
AL	All's fair in love and war.
PAUL	(*urgently*) Al, you've got to promise me that you'll leave Julie alone. You're not to get involved.
AL	Dad, it's nothing to do with you.
PAUL	It is.
AL	Why the heavy all of a sudden? You're just frightened I'm going to mess things up for you aren't you . . . with her mother?
PAUL	It's nothing to do with that. I'm just asking you . . . telling you.
AL	I'm sorry, dad, but you're not telling me anything. That's not the way we operate.

You're free to lead your life, just let me lead mine, okay? When we're at work, fair enough, you still have the last say. We're not at work now.

PAUL   Look, Al, I can't tell you why . . . not at the moment anyway. Just take my word for it, you can't go out with Julie. Why don't you just go back home and concentrate on work . . . you do that best.

AL   (*angry*) It's slave labour now is it! Do this, do that. Yes, I am good at work, but that's not everything is it? I do have a right to some free time . . . to do what I want.

PAUL   I don't want to argue with you, Al.

AL   Then just leave me alone to do my own thing. I happen to think that Julie could be the best thing that's happened to me for ages. I'm going over there.

            (AL *starts to leave*.)

PAUL   (*sharply*) Al!

AL   (*turning*) What?

PAUL   (*desperately*) Don't throw things away, Al. It's not worth it.

AL   Throw what away?

            (*During the following conversation* PAUL *occasionally clutches at his chest with a look of extreme discomfort*.)

PAUL   The business is yours, I've always said that. Maybe it's time I finished with it and let you take over. We'll arrange it whenever you like.

AL   Why? Why now?

PAUL   It's as good a time as any. I've been meaning to say something for a while, I know it's what

	you want. (*Quietly.*) There's just one condition.
AL	(*grasping the situation*) I don't go out with Julie.
PAUL	Yes.
AL	And if I do go out with Julie?
PAUL	Forget it.
AL	I can't believe I'm hearing this.
PAUL	(*sadly*) Neither can I. I once promised myself I'd never do this. (*Talking more to the plaque than to* AL.) Sometimes there's no other way of trying to get through, is there? (*To* AL.) What do you say?
AL	(*slowly, after a few seconds thought*) I've always had a lot of respect for you, dad. Do you really think that you've got to use blackmail? Why don't you just tell me the real reason behind all this?
PAUL	I can't . . . it affects other people.
AL	When you want to tell me, I'll listen. In the meantime, if you can only resort to threats, I'm not interested.
PAUL	(*desperately*) I mean it, Al . . . don't think I'm joking.
AL	Some sick joke!
PAUL	I know the business means a lot to you. I'm just asking you to do what's best for yourself.
AL	For myself, or for you! You think money rules my whole life, don't you?
PAUL	You give that impression.
AL	If it did, do you think I'd stick around in your antiquated set up? I thought you wanted me

there . . . I thought you needed me there. Obviously I was wrong, so I suggest you just stuff the business.

PAUL   You mean all this time . . . it's just been a waste!

AL   I could have done better by myself.

PAUL   You must have a pretty low opinion of me, Al. I always thought I was worth a bit more than just sympathy.

(PAUL *suddenly clutches at his chest again, inside his jacket.*)

Jesus!

AL   (*suddenly anxious*) Dad! Dad, are you okay?

PAUL   Of course I'm okay. But if I can stuff the business, you can stuff this bloody phone you make me carry about. (*Producing the phone out of his inside jacket pocket.*) Bloody aerial sticks in everywhere!

(PAUL *passes the phone to* AL.)

AL   It wasn't sympathy, dad, but I certainly didn't hang around for the money. I stayed because I love you for Christ's sake! Don't try to mess me about. You talk . . . I'll listen. Until then, you're on your own!

(AL *spins on his heels and exits left, leaving* PAUL *in despair. After a few seconds,* PAUL *makes up his mind and shouts after* AL.)

PAUL   (*shouting almost in anguish to* AL, *off*) She's your sister! (*Quietly to himself.*) Your half-sister.

(*Blackout. Music from the 1990s. When the lights rise, several days have passed. As the music fades,* PAUL *is pacing up and down as* ANNE *enters stage left.*)

ANNE	Hello, Paul.
PAUL	(*almost reluctantly*) Hi.
ANNE	No "Welcome back, how did it go"?
PAUL	(*coldly*) Welcome back, how did it go?
ANNE	Exactly as I expected . . . but thanks for asking. I thought you'd be pleased to see me back. I thought absence made the heart grow fonder.
PAUL	That all depends on what happens during the absence doesn't it?
ANNE	(*joking*) Don't tell me you've met someone else! She swept you off your feet and you're passionately in love! I bet you've got her photograph in your wallet.
PAUL	I wouldn't say swept off my feet. Knocked off my feet, maybe.
ANNE	So, do you want to stop playing games and tell me what's on your mind? Why did you want to meet me here . . . why not the caravan, or your house?
PAUL	(*angry*) Isn't that fairly obvious? Don't you think there's something we need to talk about . . . away from Julie and Al!
ANNE	(*worried*) Nothing's happened between them?
PAUL	No it hasn't . . . little thanks to you.
ANNE	Julie says she hasn't seen anything of you or Al for the last couple of days. Is that something to do with it?
PAUL	(*despairingly*) Why didn't you tell me? You should have told me.
ANNE	It is Julie isn't it?

PAUL   Of course it's Julie. Why do you think I
            warned Al off?

ANNE   Well, I hadn't noticed that she'd grown an
            extra head or anything. Warned him off what?

PAUL   All you can do is make jokes about it!

ANNE   What else can I do if you won't tell me the
            problem?

PAUL   You know the problem.

ANNE   Fine, I know the problem. Do I know the
            answer as well?

PAUL   I know who Julie is.

ANNE   So do I. She's my daughter.

PAUL   And mine.

ANNE   What!

PAUL   I had a right to know. You didn't tell me and
            I had a right to know.

ANNE   (*trying to take control*) Let's just slow down
            . . . please. Why do you think she's your
            daughter?

PAUL   It all ties up. You lie to me about her age . . .
            you lie to her about when we met, where we
            met.

ANNE   (*anxious*) Is that all?

PAUL   Isn't that enough?

ANNE   I don't think even Perry Mason would have
            been able to win with that!

PAUL   You met her father here, at a rock festival in
            1969. Julie knows that. Why tell her we met
            in the mid-60s? Why tell me she was born a
            year later than she was?

(ANNE *remains silent, thinking.*)

All this time I had a daughter and I didn't know. You won't even admit it now. I want to know why. I want to know why you decided I had no right to be involved!

ANNE   (*quietly*) Because you never were involved, in any way, shape or form.

PAUL   Because I didn't know!

ANNE   Because you're not her father.

PAUL   And that's the best you can manage? Of course I'm her father.

ANNE   Paul, you live in a world of your own . . . you invent things! You try to make the rest of the world fit into the nice little slots that suit perceptions of how your own life ought to be.

PAUL   So, why would I invent this! Do you think I want to have a daughter I've never seen until a week ago!

ANNE   I think maybe you would. It would make all your romantic notions about the last twenty-odd years actually come true wouldn't it?

PAUL   Why the lies about her age?

ANNE   Because I didn't want this situation to arise. I didn't want either Julie or you to make any connection. I didn't want either of you, both of you, to put two and two together and make five!

PAUL   So, if the answer's four, who is her father?

ANNE   It doesn't matter.

PAUL   I thought we meant something . . . I thought that back then I actually meant something to you. (*Stunned.*) You were going around with other men, weren't you!

ANNE	So, what if I was?
PAUL	You were supposed to be mine.
ANNE	Christ, you're so bloody naive! Do you really think you were that important? We were together for a week.
PAUL	You said you cared. I was faithful to you.
ANNE	Faithful to me? You married somebody else! You showed how much you cared.
PAUL	I did care. From the day we met I was always with you . . . always wanted you.
ANNE	Actions speak louder than words. All you could manage were the words.
PAUL	You were obviously better on the actions!
ANNE	I was supposed to save myself for you, was I? On the off chance that you decided there was a real person with real feelings behind that bloody stupid photograph.
PAUL	Not forever, no . . . but at least during the time we were together. Was that asking too much?
ANNE	(*close to tears*) This is stupid. I don't have to explain myself to you. Just accept that I wasn't the shining angel you seem to think I was.
PAUL	All these years I've been thinking about you. Thinking what might have been.
ANNE	Exactly. What might have been. What might have been is useless! It doesn't make you wake up in the mornings with a smile on your face. It doesn't pay tomorrow's bills. You can wish for the moon but it still stays in the sky. You stayed here and made your own life. Don't begrudge me mine!

PAUL

Yes, I made my own life. Maureen gave me everything she could . . . I gave her everything. (*Slowly.*) But I was never really happy. If I hadn't met you I could have been happy!

ANNE

I'm sorry, that's not my fault.

PAUL

Maybe not. I think you'd better go.

ANNE

Yes.

(ANNE *turns to leave as* PAUL *sits on the bench.*)

Paul.

PAUL

Yeah?

ANNE

Don't hold me responsible for your dreams.

(ANNE *again turns slowly to leave, and then stops, making a decision.*)

This is crazy . . . I can't leave like this. I don't want to leave like this.

PAUL

There's nothing to stay for.

ANNE

I don't want to hurt you. There's no reason for us to argue about things that happened so long ago. Why can't we start from here . . . start now?

PAUL

What's the point? We obviously weren't on the same wavelength then, so why should we expect anything better now?

ANNE

Maybe we know ourselves better. I did some thinking while I was away. I thought maybe there was a chance. Maybe, together, we could find some of the things we're looking for.

PAUL

I don't think that's possible now, do you?

(ANNE *slowly crosses to* PAUL *and sits by him.*)

ANNE

I haven't been entirely honest with you.

PAUL   Were you ever?

ANNE   If I tell you something, will you promise that
            you'll never tell a soul? It's important. I think
            you ought to know . . . I'd like you to know.

PAUL   (*softening*) What is it?

ANNE   You're not her father . . . but not for the
            reason I said. (*Continuing slowly and almost
            reluctantly.*) She's not my daughter either.

PAUL   What!

ANNE   Her mother was into drugs . . . When she had
            Julie she was desperate for money. She started
            dealing and got caught. Everything was going
            wrong! She knew she'd never be able to keep
            Julie . . . she was just a baby, they'd have
            taken her away. We couldn't let that happen.
            We pretended that Julie was mine.

PAUL   Why didn't you tell me this before?

ANNE   Tell you . . . I've never told anybody! Julie's
            birth certificate has me as her mother. Even
            Julie doesn't know the truth.

PAUL   But what happened to her real mother?

ANNE   She changed. Prison, more drugs . . . more
            trouble. She didn't even want to know her
            own daughter! She died when Julie was five. I
            always meant to tell Julie eventually, but . . .
            the time never seemed right. I can't tell her
            now . . . she'd never forgive me.

PAUL   Surely, she'd understand.

ANNE   I daren't take that risk. She means everything
            to me.

PAUL   I'm sorry . . . if I'd known . . .

ANNE	What was it I said the other day about honesty! You do promise you won't ever say anything, to anybody?
PAUL	(*putting his arm around* ANNE) Of course I won't. But if you'll let me, I'd like to make you think it was worth telling me the truth.
ANNE	But no rushing things.
PAUL	No rush. We've got all the time in the world.
	(PAUL *takes the phone out of his pocket.*)
ANNE	Who are you ringing?
PAUL	After the fool I've made of myself I'd like to get Scotty to beam me up! I think I should tell Al he hasn't got a half-sister after all.
ANNE	You told him?
PAUL	I had to. He had his beady eye on Julie! I thought he'd throw a fit . . . storm off, I don't know. Do you know what he said?
ANNE	What?
PAUL	He just said, "You randy old bugger".
ANNE	If you ring now, you might disappoint him.
PAUL	(*dialling*) I think he ought to know, don't you?
ANNE	This could be wonderful. You and me . . . Julie and Al.
PAUL	I think you're incredible. Taking on somebody else's child like that.
ANNE	It just felt right. I never regretted it.
PAUL	Somebody from the commune?
ANNE	Not quite! You remember Shirley?
PAUL	Shirley!

ANNE   My twin sister. Julie was hers.

                     (PAUL, *looking shocked, quickly puts the
                     phone back in his pocket.*)

                     No answer?

PAUL   Er . . . no.

ANNE   Poor Shirley. I said the other day that a lot of
                     us just played at being hippies. Not Shirley. It
                     ended up being more than a game for her.

                     (PAUL *stands silently and moves away from*
                     ANNE.)

                     What's the matter?

PAUL   Nothing.

                     (ANNE *follows him.*)

ANNE   Does it shock you? That I can't tell Julie
                     about my own twin sister?

PAUL   No, it's not that. I just think we may have a
                     problem.

ANNE   What problem?

PAUL   I don't know if you remember, but on the first
                     day we ever met you said something about
                     you and Shirley sharing everything. I can
                     remember because at the time it sounded
                     incredibly generous.

ANNE   So?

PAUL   (*slowly and cautiously*) There's something I
                     think you need to know about Shirley and
                     me . . .

                     *The lights fade as music of the late 1960s
                     plays.*

FURNITURE AND PROPERTY LIST

ACT ONE

Scene One

Set
Bench with plaque
Signpost (1996 version)

Offstage
Sports bag containing mobile phone, rug and newspaper (PAUL)

Personal
Handkerchief (PAUL)
Wallet containing photograph (PAUL)

Scene Two

Strike
Bench

Set
Signpost (1969 version)

Offstage
Large handbag containing pencil (OLIVE)
Bag containing flask, cups, newspaper, binoculars, and pullover (OLIVE)
Two deck chairs
Bag containing packs of sandwiches and Battenburg cake (PAUL)
Rug (PAUL)
Shells wrapped in scarf (ANNE)

Personal
Handkerchief (OLIVE)

ACT TWO

Scene One

Strike
Deck chairs
Bags and all contents

Set
Large bag (page 62)

Personal   Joint (PAUL)
            Foil wrapper (PAUL)
            Small medicine bottle containing pills
            (ALBERT)
            Camera (PAUL)

Scene Two

Strike   Bag
            Signpost (1969 version)

Set   Bench with plaque
            Signpost (1996 version)
            Picnic hamper containing bottle of wine,
            corkscrew and tumblers
            Open bottle of wine (one quarter full)
            Food
            Tumblers

Offstage   Sticking plaster (PAUL)

Personal   Watch (PAUL)
            Mobile phone (PAUL)

LIGHTING PLOT

All scenes effect of bright sunshine. Lights fading between
scenes and sub-scenes.

EFFECTS PLOT

Cue 1   PAUL ". . . make it up as you go along."   Page 6
        Mobile phone rings

Cue 2   *The lights rise . . .*   Page 8
        Mobile phone rings

Cue 3   ANNE ". . . couple of weeks with her friend." Page 17
        Mobile phone rings

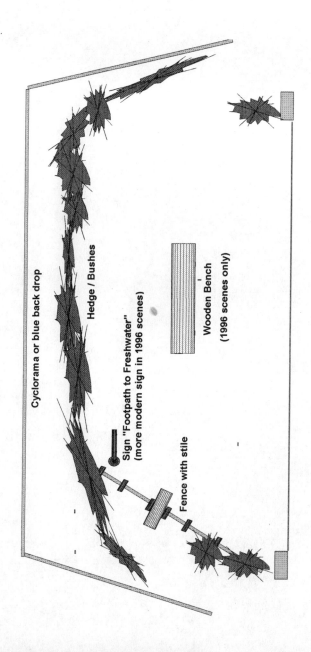

Cyclorama or blue back drop

Hedge / Bushes

Sign "Footpath to Freshwater"
(more modern sign in 1996 scenes)

Fence with stile

Wooden Bench
(1996 scenes only)